Called into Ministry

To Be a Good and Faithful Pastor

Reflections of a Partnered Lesbian

by Mary Albing

Kirk House Publishers
Minneapolis, Minnesota

Called into Ministry

To Be a Good and Faithful Pastor

Reflections of a Partnered Lesbian

by Mary Albing

Albing, Mary
Called into ministry : to be a good and faithful pastor : reflections of a partnered lesbian.
p. cm.
Includes bibliographic references
ISBN 1-886513-94-5 (alk. paper)
1. Lutheran Church—United States—Clergy—Biography. 2. Lesbian clergy—United States—Biography. I. Title.

BX8080.A36 A3 2004
284.1/092 B 22

2004062400

Kirk House Publishers, PO Box 390759, Minneapolis, Minnesota 55439
Manufactured in the United States of America

Contents

Preface

Mary Albing is my pastor, and I am grateful.

She came into our midst announcing that she wants to be a pastor and not join a debate. As you will discover in this book, she feels deeply the call to ministry.

Pastor Albing is an excellent preacher. Her sermons are clear and well crafted. Those included here illustrate her consistent proclamation of the Gospel.

Throughout the book are portraits of Mary's relationship to people that portray her intense interest in and love for those in her care. Her chapter on compassion is particularly compelling. The stories from her ministry reveal a pastor with an authentic compassion for those in her parish.

She writes, "...the times we have the most trouble acting on another person's suffering, and times we are judgmental are the times we feel most at risk and the times we are most afraid to look at ourselves...."

This is not just the story of ministry, nor is it a simple story of parish pastor. Mary is a lesbian. Her ministry has a personal side. She tells about leaving her husband, of her relationship with her two children. There is pain and trauma, joy and freedom in her account of achieving what she believes God created her to be. Resigning from parish ministry, she served as a hospital chaplain and found that her time serving the great needs of others was a time of growth and healing for herself, too.

Mary accepted a call to our parish; it was not an officially sanctioned call. To Mary it is worth the risk because her heart and soul are in parish ministry.

And, our congregation? Membership grows steadily. Sunday school and youth ministry have improved. Worship is done with dignity and delight. Our facilities have been renovated. Our pastor reaches out with ease to young and old, to persons of varied backgrounds.

Mary Albing is my pastor, and I am very grateful!

L. David Brown, Retired Bishop
Evangelical Lutheran Church in America

Introduction

This is my reflection on my ministry as a lesbian Lutheran pastor. I have written it because the Lutheran church, which I love, is so deeply divided on the issue of homosexuality and the place of homosexual persons in the church. The argument has created a great deal of frustration and confusion. On the one side, some cannot understand how anyone could even think about having a gay pastor. Many read the Bible as plainly saying homosexuality is sinful. On the other side are those who cannot understand what the problem is. In their eyes the Bible does not address the current situation. In the middle are a great number of people confused by the voices on both sides. They simply want a good and faithful pastor in their own congregations.

This book is an attempt to broaden the conversation. I have written this book because the homosexuality debate is about me, a partnered lesbian who simply wishes to serve in the denomination in which I was born and nurtured, and in which I find the most meaning for my faith and life. I serve in the ways that countless others have served before me. I preach, teach, administer the sacraments, and comfort those who are grieving. So this is one person's story of being called into ministry. All the anecdotal narratives here are true. Names and many circumstances have been changed to protect the privacy of individuals.

Following each chapter is a sermon, related to the theme of the previous chapter. Most of these I've preached during the my first year at Lutheran Church of Christ the Redeemer. My call is to Word and Sacrament ministry. I cannot share my worship life in this format, but I can share a portion of how I preach.

Many thanks go to Leonard Flachman, who invited me to write this story and supported me in many ways, and to Rev. Tim Thorstenson for his invaluable suggestions and patient encouragement. Many friends have given their moral support and I am grateful. I include among them Bob Albing and members of my congregation, Lutheran Church of Christ the Redeemer. My children, Dan and Hannah, are always my cheerleaders. My deepest gratitude is to Jane Lien, my life companion, who has more faith in me and my work than I'll ever have in myself, and who shares with me love and hope for the church.

Called into Hearing

A Sunday school teacher asked her class of kindergartners about their concerns. Little Jimmy was worried about his grandmother. She had arthritis and in the cold weather she hurt everywhere. When everyone had a chance to share, the teacher invited them to pray about whatever they liked. So when Jimmy's turn came he prayed, "Dear Jesus, make it hot for Grandma." – Elsie's favorite joke.

There is a stretch of road that reaches west from Hannaford, North Dakota. Elsie, one of my first parishioners, lived on a farm out this way. The first length is paved. Exactly one mile out of town is a set of tracks where the Great Northern Railroad crosses. Beyond the tracks the road surface changes to gravel and leads to places one cannot see. Hardly a tree or barn breaks the horizon. In the summer, the roadside is green with wheat and sunflowers. By late July the huge flowers uniformly face east like a very large congregation standing and awaiting a blessing. The fall shrivels them and turns them brown and the seeds blacken their countenance. The wheat flows with the wind, the color of the tow-headed children in the little town. The winter, with fields tilled and covered with snow is barren, as though God, who wetted a finger and wiped the earth with green and goodness, has turned away leaving a great chill. Late in the evening, the trains approaching the crossing hoot a long, haunting warning. When we lived there, we knew it was 11 o'clock and time to sleep.

The mile to the railroad track was well traveled with the tennis shoes of heart patients and people like me, a little overweight after the birth of my second child. Every morning at 7:30, provided it was above twenty degrees, I walked along the shoulder of the paved road. Sometimes I met others along the way. Sometimes my husband, Bob, went along. Mostly I walked alone. After living there for a few weeks, Shag, the springer spaniel who lived next door, caught on to my routine and nearly always joined me. Dogs, like the rest of us, love ritual. He ran through the tall grass or snow, snuffling for mice, or in the deep of summer, chasing dragonflies. We had a picture directory of all of the members of the congregations we were serving as pastors. It was not that many—two or three hundred souls. I took a page from a church directory along on the walk and prayed for each one on it and their families.

We knew, it seemed, everything about them. Their birthdays and how their families celebrated them. Whether or not their bread had risen that week or failed. Where their relatives lived, even distant ones, and we had met almost all of them. When a daughter was expecting a baby or when the pigs were farrowing we heard about it. We knew what kind of crops they raised and had walked through some of their barns and fields. We knew their favorite recipes and what kind of dressing they liked on their salads. And we knew that some of their salads involved little marshmallows and whipped cream. As I walked along, I could pray for their hopes and losses. We knew everything about them, and yet we did not always understand one another.

Sometimes when I walked with others they let me in on the town gossip. Nobody liked the former pastor in a nearby parish. "How come?" I asked.

"He was henpecked."

"What do you mean?"

"You know what henpecked means, don'cha?"

"Yes, but how do you know he was henpecked?"

"Well, you know the guy is henpecked if he's out in the back yard hanging up sheets."

"And underwear," his friend chimed in.

"Can you believe it? And she doesn't even have a job, but just one kid. She sits in the house with the kid, drinking coffee and he's having to hang up their underwear, for all the world to see. Sheesh."

On a trip home I picked up a large antique buffet from my grandmother's house. We put it in a U-Haul trailer and dragged it across two states. We arrived at our parsonage at 11:30 at night, exhausted. No lights were on in any of the homes around us and no one was about. We opened our garage door, backed the trailer in, unhitched the car and closed the door in a matter of seconds. The next morning before eight o'clock two people came to the door asking what was under the tarp on the trailer in our garage.

The residents of Hannaford were used to living in the fishbowl of a small town and adjusted in various ways. Those who had lived there all their lives already knew the stories and already knew the unspoken rules about living there. Elsie had grown up in the far away, exotic city of Milwaukee. She had been a caterer and met her future husband, a wealthy farmer, there. He swept her off her feet and brought her back to rural Hannaford. She was an avid gardener and a gracious entertainer who fed the birds and deer in her large yard, and collected antique cut glass and cats. When I met her she was in her eighties, still had some red hair that she never colored, and was very spry. Her husband had died some years before. She insisted I come out to her farm to visit her. What followed in the course of the conversation was a dance to figure out whether I approved of people drinking a little wine. Soon after, she wondered if I could take her to Jamestown, 60 miles away. I did, and in this way one of the pastors of the Lutheran parish in Hannaford came to conspire with one of its most affluent members to buy her wine.

Elsie and I made regular trips to Jamestown in my elderly brown Bonneville. She was dependent on rides from others since her husband died. She did not want to buy her underwear anywhere where someone would comment on the size or color. She certainly did not want to buy liquor anywhere near home either, because tongues would wag. So we would travel the sixty miles. I would run into the liquor store, with the car still running, and get a bottle of wine for her. One day she turned to me and said, "Not all the pastors have done this for me." Then we would shop at a local department store and pick up the things that were too personal to get near home.

In many insignificant ways we differed from residents there. I enjoyed my large back yard and with help from a local farmer dug a vegetable garden in the back. Tim roared into the back yard with a diesel tractor, tilled it with a couple of passes of a large implement, then came back with a dump truck with aged manure. Another neighbor came over and tilled it with his heavy garden tiller. Presto, I had a magnificent garden.

I planted it with corn and radishes, broccoli and tomatoes, and spinach and cucumbers, and edged it with marigolds and nasturtiums. I laid newspapers and yard bags between the rows for mulch. Soon a neighbor asked what I was doing. His garden, with its perfect rows and lovely tilled soil between, never had one weed and I never saw him in it. All summer, with a twinkle in his eye, he gave me grief about putting garbage between the rows of my garden.

The smallest details became everyone's business. But that was also true in larger congregations and in other places. Hannaford was just a good example of what was true for most of our ministry. We came to know one another; our strengths and weaknesses quickly became obvious to all. In kind communities and congregations our errors and ignorance were overlooked. In Hannaford we were invited to birthdays, baptismal celebrations, favorite restaurants and ball games.

At the same time that we were invited into the community, into celebrations, into families and their lives, we were still in many ways outsiders and had outsiders' perspectives. From that vantage point, some of what happened in that community was at first baffling. We thought we were worldlier, more perceptive, and in fact because we had a different lens on every day life there, it was true to some extent. Newcomers always see a community in a fresh way.

We lived in Madagascar for a year. We took the most pictures and wrote our most insightful and detailed journal entries in the first few weeks we were there. We spent hours describing how startlingly red the soil is against the green of the trees and the drab colors of the homes stacked into the hillsides of the capital city, Antananarivo, how beautiful and charming the manners, skin and dress of the people. How wonderful the busy, clattering open markets were, the streets jammed with umbrellas and people. Later when we made friends there, the more remarkable and memorable parts of our experiences were relationships, and what we had in common with the Malagasy who, though different from us in many ways, shared similar hopes and dreams and faith.

We had some insights simply because we were new to Hannaford. Travelers to distant cultures take their best pictures and make their best and freshest observations before they become a part of it, but they also miss a great deal. Every place, including that little town in North Dakota, has its own special vernacular. Language and dialects aside, each community has a set of common experiences that give rise to humor and pain. They have inside jokes and shared grief. Certain people interact in certain ways with others that are common knowledge to all but the newest members of the community. Some are friends or bitter enemies. Social strata dictate some customs, courtesies or disrespect. Somebody will make a funny little public error that people don't forget for years. Someone makes a remark that is never forgiven. Someone comes up on the short end of the family inheritance and in every meeting where both families are present a power struggle ensues. Not having this inside information, not knowing the stories, becomes a trap or an obstacle course for newcomers trying to make friends or interact on a professional level.

It is easy to be critical of the way people live, whether rural or urban or somewhere in between. It is much more interesting to love people just the way they come. That is the key to being contented wherever we are. We can learn to relish the differences. Early on in my life I worried so much about whether I looked like a good teacher or pastor that I missed learning about the people and the joy of simply being there. I worried so much about fitting in and getting it right, or worse, them getting it right, that I did not claim my particular place in that community, the place to which I had been called. I had to put myself in their shoes and think about how much I would like to be heard in order to hear them in a deep way. I finally was called into hearing not only what people said but also what they meant.

The first time I went to a meeting of the women's group at Eidfjord Lutheran Church, they were all sitting around the table in the kitchen. They had their coats on and the large oven door laid open. It was below zero outside, this January afternoon, and it was much more efficient just heating the kitchen rather than trying to heat the whole church. A dozen ladies looked up at me expectantly as I came in the door.

The chairwoman was energetic and very well organized. She had a booklet of their membership, a schedule of meetings, and chosen ministries. But I noticed something nearly right away. The membership list was alphabetical and organized by their husbands' names and last names: for example, Mrs. Alfred Anderson. I had met a few of them on Sunday and recognized most of their faces. But I had met at least two hundred people and could not remember many names. So I greeted them and told them I was happy that they had invited me, that I was looking forward to leading the study and I'd like to get to know their names as soon as possible. I asked for their help with that.

The chairwoman said, "Well, you have a list of our names."

I complimented her on it and said, "I just don't know which one belongs to whom." So each one told me the name listed in the booklet.

"So is that what you would like me to call you?" They all looked at one another as if they were thinking, What have we done? What odd creature are we stuck with now? I tried to make myself understood. "Do you want me to call you Mrs. Paul, or do you want me to call you by your given name, Dorothy?"

"Oh," they said together and smiled, and again they looked at each other, this time with great relief on their faces.

I understood much about them. I grew up in a congregation that was literally surrounded by cornfields: Delafield Lutheran, near Wilder, Minnesota. The intimate gathering of women in the basement was not strange to me, only their formality. Where I grew up, we all called one another by our first names. Even children called adults by their first names. For me, the Eidfjord women's manner of introducing themselves for the first time was a sign that the women were lost somehow in their husbands' identities. I was raised in the 60's and 70's in the midst of the feminist movement, and I got my training at seminary and in an urban congregation, Our Saviour's in Minneapolis, among self-identified feminists—teachers, business owners, story-tellers, musicians and social workers. But out here on these snowy plains, I wondered what sense the women had of themselves.

I learned that married women's identities were as they expressed, close to their husbands. They worked side by side with their husbands, owned businesses with them, farmed with them, kept the home fires burning. That was how it was done. Not too many women were independently employed outside their homes. At any rate, there weren't that many places to be employed, even if they wanted to be, so the family farm or restaurant was their business, and their husband's well-being really was their well-being. In this rural area where I served, the men and women were a team, even though the women occupied a lower social status in some respects, as women often do. Strong willed, often vocal and opinionated, yet their identities were unashamedly connected with others—husbands and children, but also with their schools, churches and towns. They recognized their interdependence though they might not have named it. Younger people were less bound to older customs, though strong boundaries were drawn around certain kinds of work. Still, family identity was very strong.

It is not always easy to tell our stories, and our stories are sometimes difficult to hear. Elsie's mail had come. She was sorting through it in the kitchen as we drank coffee one day. A letter had come that said "Elsie Williams" on it. She held it out for me to see. And in a plaintive voice she said, "I hate getting mail like this. It reminds me that I'm a widow." Having Herbert's name on her mail kept a part of his spirit with her. This is what I had missed from the beginning.

The strip of North Dakota along Highway 1 was settled by sincere pietists in the mid to late 1800s. Drinking, dancing, smoking and playing cards were strongly discouraged. Vestiges of their beliefs still come out mainly in concerns about drinking. Drinking alcohol is frowned upon by the pious, even though in most little towns there may only be a grocery store, a gas station and a bar. In one of the congregations we served, a local bar owner began coming to church only a few years before. He had been told for years that he was not welcome.

It is not always easy to tell our stories, and they are sometimes difficult to hear. One day a woman I didn't recognize came to the house. It was early on a sultry morning. I hadn't left for the day yet. She knocked on the front door, which no one ever used. It was a sure sign that she was a stranger. No one in town would ever use the front door. They came to the side door near the kitchen. Some came in with barely a knock, though everyone was sure to knock after a man once walked in on me wearing just my skivvies. She said in a rush, "I know you don't know me. My name is Carol. I know you, and I've seen you around, and I've heard about you." She named her town, several miles away. "And I would just like to talk to you for five minutes."

I invited her into our office and we sat down. Red-faced and sweating she said, "I don't want to waste your time. Sorry. I'm leaving my husband." I sympathized with her and asked her if there was anything we could do. Would she and her husband like to meet with Bob or me? She said it was too late for that. "He hits me. Only when he drinks... But I can't do nothing about that and he'll never change. I have my bags packed and I'm ready to go." She pointed out the window. Her car was full of things and was running. "I just wanted to let someone know that I was leaving so if they start to look for me, they'll know that nothing bad happened to me."

I asked if she knew where she was going, what she was doing, with whom she would stay. Did she need help? She said she didn't have a plan except that she was going to school. She just wanted one person to know, and she had decided that since I was a woman and a pastor who was sworn to keep her secrets, she could tell me and I would understand. I promised to pray for her. I thought of all she had been through, and all that was ahead, how courageous she was, and how so many women never get away. Her eyes filled with tears, she grasped my hand tightly, and then said, "I know this isn't the best way, but the best way isn't going to happen and I can't stand it anymore." Then she hurried out the door. Belatedly I wondered how I would know if they were looking for her.

I watched the newspapers and listened to town gossip in case the police began looking for her. She was in my dreams for weeks, with all the different scenarios of helping her and her husband. Her story was hard to hear. But I couldn't make it better. She was wiser than I was and more courageous.

The early settlers were not stupid. They came by their pietism honestly. People might drink to battle the dark, and in midwinter on the frosty, windswept prairies, it's bitterly cold nearly all the time. Alcohol, a powerful drug, can make the afflicted forget their problems for a time. A strong prohibition became the norm because alcohol abuse pulls apart the community with loss of work, loss of relationships and even death. We disliked the "blue" laws, but some of these customs have much deeper origins than convenience or superficial piety. They combat the loss of the soul.

We were called into listening deeply to people's stories and entering into their experience by their rules. I discovered that when we think that the places or people we are watching are simple, it is a plain sign that we are blinded by our parochialism, that we simply do not understand what is really happening. In that small community where I lived as a pastor I learned about the subtlety and complexity of communication and resolved to listen to the subtext of individuals and the whole community without being judgmental. I learned to enter into their places on their terms more quickly and hear their wisdom about themselves. That paid off many times in the years that followed.

It is not always easy to tell our stories, and they are sometimes difficult to hear. When I was 40 years old I realized that I was lesbian. I had been married for 12 years. For many years I had gay friends, had worked out for myself many of the issues that still trouble the church. I had a sense that God would never reject me on account of creating me this way. I felt different, but not condemned. Still I was isolated, afraid, and wounded. I thought I surely must be mistaken. I was also overwhelmed with guilt about the pain I would cause family and friends. I prayed and was comforted with meditation and music, but I knew I could not bear this burden alone. My first challenge was finding someone I could tell. Some of the people I was closest to, some of the most gracious, generous and lovely people I knew at the time could not hear me, or at least I was afraid they could not.

Some had identified themselves to me years earlier in plain terms. I remember several years ago sitting at dinner with close family friends and Janet. I knew how much she sometimes had to endure. Her mother made life as difficult for Janet as possible. She was rude and critical to Janet, the only person who supported her. Still Janet loved her, spent as much time with her as she could, provided for her financially, made her as comfortable as possible, and tried to show her respect even in the midst of faultfinding and criticism. We often talked together about things her mother said, her disaffection, and her ability to diminish Janet's every word and action. Her experience with her mother strengthened her to reach out to others in the community. Bright, interested in politics and literature, Janet could talk with me about anything.

But at this dinner she began to say terribly judgmental things about homosexuals, and to ask all kinds of questions about how they could even have sex. How do they do it? She wondered if I knew. Though amusing, after this kind of conversation the topic was off the table forever. After participating in this conversation, even though it happened years earlier, there was no way I would ever disclose to her anything about myself. I knew that she could not hear it.

Even those close to me, who had many gay friends, were difficult to confide in. I chose to tell a friend who lived in another part of the country. She was well-meaning but told me that I needed to stay in closer contact. She went on for some time about the great difficulties of her other lesbian friends and then said, "You can't just unload a problem like this on someone and not stay in touch so that I know you're OK." Suddenly I had a problem so enormous that I needed to be in constant contact with her. I didn't tell another soul for many months, because if it was so terrible for another professional to hear, who could possibly bear this burden with me? Now I was not only weighed down by my own sense of shock, and the fear and shame of being different, but also the sense that I would be burdening anyone I told.

I told my husband, Bob, who was devastated, but kind. We could not really help one another, except to be kind, and I no longer knew who was safe to tell. So at least at first I would be as certain as possible that the person I was talking to would be understanding toward me, and that I could be fairly positive of getting a good reception. It also had to be an exceptionally strong person. I wasn't about to lay my burden on anyone else. No one around the edges of my life needed to know. Only those who would care for me and those who needed to know for legal and professional reasons.

In this way many of my roads to help were blocked. Not too many people unknowingly passed the test of being both open to my discovery and at the same time pragmatic, downplaying it enough to make it seem like ordinary human behavior. Like being redheaded or dark skinned. Something noticeable and yet an ordinary characteristic of the human race.

After a few years I went into chaplaincy, and among those who serve the most vulnerable and wounded, I found the open solace of God. The chaplains I worked with unaccountably and immediately could not only hear the painful stories I told, but welcomed them. I soon understood how they could hold that perspective as I met one patient after another who felt their stories were too difficult for their loved ones. Everyone has a "coming out" story, something they wish others didn't know about or care about. They tired of telling the same story over and over. They worried that loved ones would think less of them, that they might lose even more than they had already lost, that their loved ones would reject them. Through my own experience of longing to be heard, God called me into hearing them.

Don was suffering severe pain in his back. Multiple myeloma had chewed holes into his bones. He was yelling. As chaplain I had talked with him several times, so I stopped into his room just in time to hear him fire a young resident physician. She was reasoning with him. He sat backwards in a straight chair, like a cowboy on a horse, bracing himself against the back. His face was shiny with sweat and stretched tight in his agony. A thin, pale tube connected him to a bag hanging on a metal tree. He was holding a small cup containing little white tablets with a shaking hand. In the other hand he held an emesis basin. "Get out!" he shouted at the resident who stood with her arms folded in front of her. "And don't you come back either." She gave up and left. I began to back out too.

"Don't you dare leave me!" he said to me. "Don't you dare. If you leave me, you are no kind of pastor."

I put my arm across his shoulder. "I won't go. What's the problem?" I asked.

"She doesn't listen." He was slurring the words together.

"That is a problem around here," I agreed. I sat next to him.

"Honey, that ain't the only problem."

"What do you mean?" I thought he was going to complain about the hospital.

He told me about the night before. They were changing his medication to these tablets so that he could go home. He got disoriented in the middle of the night, walked around the room trying to find the bathroom. He soiled himself while he was trying to find it. And then he fell. His wife was there. She tried to help him up off the floor and clean him up. He refused to have staff come in, though finally an aide prevailed. Just then his son came in, a fire fighter. "He saw me like that. He cleaned me up and picked me up like a baby and put me in my bed. Just like a baby."

"How awful for you. You were humiliated."

"Yes, I was. This is terrible, just terrible."

I stayed with him quietly. He asked for water. I reached over to his tray. He emptied the pills in his mouth and swallowed them with a gulp of water and gave the glass back to me.

"But you know, that wasn't the worst part." I sat wondering how it could get much worse. His story was hard to follow because his speech was slurred and from time to time he had to throw up. "I was in Vietnam."

"What did you do there?"

"I was a paratrooper. It was nuts. We'd jump down into that tall grass and we just knew there were Cong down there hiding, just waiting to pick us off when we jumped. They sent us in there and people all around were shot while they were suspended in the air. They died before they hit the ground."

"You've been in awful situations before."

"Damn right. Here's the thing. I was hit. Right in the back."

"You're kidding! And you lived to tell about it."

"Yeah, I was hit, see? And when I hit the ground I pulled off my pack and hollered for the medic. It was crazy. People were running and shooting and it was so loud. Unbelievable. And I looked at my pack, 'cause I didn't feel anything. But sure enough. It had a hole in it and blood all over it. I yelled, 'I've been hit! I've been hit!' And the medic ran over and checked me over. He looked and looked and couldn't find nothing. And then he opened my pack. It was ketchup. They shot my ketchup but my rations stopped the bullet. And I cried!" Don began to sniffle now. I got him the box of tissues and he howled, "Oh, God! I cried like a baby." I sat quietly with my arm across his shoulders. I heard him.

"You're afraid and don't want to be a coward."

"That's it, you know, for my son. He needs me. He still needs me."

I heard him and he knew it. And when I heard him, I also knew what to say. I reminded him that he had been courageous before. He had practice in being courageous in life threatening situations. Yes, he had been afraid when he jumped into the jungle, knowing that he could be killed at any moment. Sometimes fear is a smart thing. When there is actual danger, fear is smart, a gift, and not something to condemn. But in spite of his fear he had accomplished what needed to be done. I guessed that there were many other times in his life when he had needed courage and found it. He agreed, and we talked together about how God would give him what he needed now.

We are called into hearing one another by the one who always hears us, who told us that if we knock, the door would open to us (Luke 11:9). We are heard whenever we dare to speak by the Holy One. But when we can hear one another it is a lovely thing. When we can learn to do so without being judgmental or afraid, it is a great gift, because it calls from us all the good things of which God makes us capable.

Sermon • November 28, 2003

In those days and at that time I will cause a righteous Branch to spring up for David; and he shall execute justice and righteousness in the land (Jeremiah 33:15).

When I was just a little kid and some small motor or appliance broke, my dad took it to Jack. He lived on a farm about three miles away, and if something was fixable, he could fix it.

Sometimes, if it happened that I was somewhere in the vicinity, I got to tag along. We'd go in my dad's old Ford pickup. I loved to ride with my dad in his pickups. The cabs smelled of grain, grease and his pipe smoke. There was usually an old *Time* magazine, or something else that had fallen and slid under the seat, for the slow times when we were waiting.

I loved going to Jack's. He was short and round and square jawed and gave us "the business." He had a shop that looked like a junkyard. I don't know how he ever found anything. It was dark in his shop, and there were greasy, dirty piles of stuff everywhere. Old mufflers leaned on the wall. A pile of tires lay there, along with used car batteries. Long and short, fat and thin wires of various colors and lengths hung on nails on the wall. Spray cans of lubricant sat on 50 gallon barrels of various things. There were tools, large bolts and burrs, metal shafts with interesting cogs, and always, always on top of some pile there was a Tupperware of homemade donuts. Jack's wife didn't send him out to his shop to starve. He told stories, long and amusing. And then he'd spit, which we found fascinating and disgusting. Dad complained that Jack couldn't just fix something and get it over with.

Dad had to complain, you see, because Jack was German. He wasn't really. His grandparents immigrated at about the time my dad's did. But dad called him a German.

And there was still a sort of friendly rivalry between the German Lutherans and the Norwegian Lutherans. The Norwegians were messy and didn't work as hard as they did, the Germans said. And the Norwegians thought the Germans drank too much beer. Both were probably a little bit right, at least in our neighborhood. But Jack could make things work and my dad was not one to just throw things away if they could be fixed.

> *In those days and at that time I will cause a righteous Branch to spring up for David; and he shall execute justice and righteousness in the land.*

In Old Testament terms, Jack executed righteousness. He made things work. If it's righteous, it works. Righteousness isn't a moral characteristic, or the state of being right, as in correct, or knowledgeable. Maybe words that come close to it in our culture would be mature or wise, not in attaining a certain age, but in taking responsibility for things working well in our communities, especially in relationships. Mature or wise persons help others get along better, they are less and less aware of self and more of neighbors, they protect and defend those who have less and are at risk in some way. They fear God in the most basic senses. They make things work. Of course, hoping for one like this to arise, as Jeremiah says, *a righteous branch, one who will execute justice and righteousness*, implies that he or she is needed.

Today is the first day of the church year. In Advent we begin to prepare for the coming of Christ. We can see that the world around us is preparing for Christmas. But we take just a moment at the beginning, to allow ourselves the space to acknowledge our anguish over the world as it is and hope for a time when the whole creation is as God first intended. We give rise to our hopes for the Christ to come again, because the Christ is needed.

Where our weariness, sorrow, fear, sense of abandonment or sense of being trapped become very intense, and where we expect things to be get better, there is anguish. This community is one of the only places where we are allowed to express our anguish publicly. We Americans are very "can do." We believe that we're going to solve problems once and for all and that there will be no more anguish in need of caring ministry and healing. So we don't seem to have the ability to talk publicly about what is painful or frightening without raising our voices at one another. We don't talk well about our anguish, so we raise our voices at one another about war, abortion, the environment, our enormous national debt and gay rights. We can't talk about our painful spiritual losses or the way all of these things affect real people all the time. We just raise our voices, withdraw, get depressed or become indifferent to mask our knowledge and anguish that things aren't working. Unrighteousness abounds.

The same thing happens at work. Our work can provide us with great satisfaction and purpose. But some of you have told me about your extreme anguish that your work situations have caused you. You are experiencing a loss of meaning. Justice is not being done. People are suffering, losing sleep, losing their homes. Someone, or the system, is taking away something—yours or another's dignity, freedom or sense of purpose. Most people take jobs thinking they will love them, and many of you love your work. When it goes badly in some way you experience a fundamental loss. Your loss causes genuine anguish. This is repeated over and over in work places all around. Why do we not talk about the anguish of one half of our waking hours? We just raise our voices, withdraw, get depressed or become indifferent. Things aren't working. Unrighteousness abounds.

This same anguish is in our homes. We are allowed to grieve for about three days in our culture, and then we are supposed to get over it. And our sorrow is really only supposed to be over very close friends or relatives. There are very few things about which we are allowed to be upset. So we cover it up. We get angry and act out, withdraw, become depressed or indifferent. Things aren't working. Unrighteousness abounds.

This is why we have this first Sunday in Advent. Could we just acknowledge our collective anguish as human beings?

One of my favorite movies is *As Good as It Gets.* Jack Nicholson is a romance novel writer. He's written dozens of these cheesy books and is now very wealthy. But he has a problem. He has obsessive-compulsive disorder. He counts everything. He avoids cracks in the sidewalk. He is obsessed by the thought of someone else's germs. His life has shrunk down into a tiny world between his apartment and one restaurant, in which he insists on sitting at a certain table, ordering the exact same food from the exact same server with his own plasticware that he brings with him from home. He is mean-spirited and self-centered, and he drives everyone crazy because he is obnoxious to anyone who gets in the way of his needed routine.

During the course of the movie, and through some odd coincidences, he falls in love with the woman who has been serving him in the restaurant every day. His hopes are very high, but his behavior is so erratic that she insists that he get help. In the end they get together, but only after he comes to terms with himself. The movie's title comes from the turning point in the movie. He bursts into a room of his long-suffering therapist's patients and in his anguish demands, "What if this is as good as it gets?"

Well, it just can't be, and so we have the hopeful strains of scripture:

In those days and at that time I will cause a righteous Branch to spring up for David; and he shall execute justice and righteousness in the land.

Someday the world as we know it will end and righteousness will abound. Things will work as they should. People will treat one another as they ought. Christ is in the future. But in the meantime, God has given us a way to prepare for Christ's coming and it is the very thing that troubles us: our anguish. In our anguish lies the spiritual meaning and energy to embrace and to heal and finally to transcend our circumstances and to take on a position of preparation and hope. Our anguish doesn't have to defeat us. It is the path by which we become mature and wise, the path by which we connect deeply and most meaningfully with others, the path that energizes us to look beyond ourselves.

Jack's last years were filled with sorrow. His son was killed in a car accident when he was in his twenties. His wife fell into grief and soon after died of cancer. At some point, I realized that my dad was going over there with the littlest things. A plastic fan, the motor from the microwave that makes the plate turn around. Not to get things fixed anymore, but because Jack was out there alone on his place. One day, Dad had him fixing even the toaster when it had truly and thoroughly died a little electronic death. Jack fixed it, told his stories, spat, I'm sure, and told my dad that he couldn't talk about even the weather without crying anymore. "An old man's disability," he told him.

It would be wrong to say that Dad and Jack weren't waiting for a better world to come. They were. But in that relationship, where anguish was shared for a moment, and where Jack made some small thing right for just a while, one small thing, a bit of the preparation of the world in God was completed. Soon, I would think they would both say. Soon and very soon.

Called into Compassion

A man on a horse would be too far away and a blind man wouldn't care. – Elsie, about a mistake I made when I was quilting.

I walked into the spacious kitchen of a large church. A dozen volunteers were gathered around a stainless steel island on tall stools buttering large piles of buns for a reception for three hundred. I enjoyed talking to them and we often joked as they worked. "Laura," I said to one woman as I walked behind her, "I think you missed a spot." I expected her to laugh, but she huffed and pointed at another woman, "I'm tired of being criticized. Judy already told me that!" she said and her eyes filled with tears. I apologized, saying I was only meaning to tease her. Her surprising revelation of her hurt stopped the chatting for a moment. The women were quiet and uncomfortable. Then Betty, still buttering the bun in her hands, began to talk about how they needed to be kinder to one another, how her feelings had also been hurt recently by thoughtless criticism. Judy apologized to Laura. The conversation became light again.

Our perfectionism can harden our hearts toward others and make our tasks burdensome. We endure constant slights from one another, often unintended. We usually feel that we don't measure up in some arena in our lives and do not need to be reminded. We often already have an old tape in our head from someone in the family criticizing us, telling us some old message about how we look or act that is not acceptable. Even as adults, one little word can fell us.

I stood with kids and parents on a cold spring morning in a church parking lot as they gathered for a youth event. Three volunteers were driving them a few miles away. We were standing in a large ring, talking and laughing. Frost edged the lot and a little fog accompanied each comment or laugh. One of the kids stood without a coat and bounced up and down rubbing his arms. Sara's cell phone rang. It was Jennifer, one of the drivers. She would be a little late. Sara, who was organizing the event, rolled her eyes. "She is always late."

No one paid much attention, but we were all getting chilly. Fifteen minutes later her phone rang again. Sara talked quietly, then sidled over to me. "Is anything wrong?" I asked.

"She said she has to drive Joe in for medical tests, but she thinks Ray, her brother-in-law, will drive for her. I don't know why Joe can't just drive himself! He's such a baby! And Jennifer should have known this. Why didn't she just ask Ray in the first place? She's so disorganized." Sara began to complain about Jennifer and Joe, her husband. I stopped her, saying I could understand her frustration and was sure that Jennifer had a good reason for being late. "Yes. But we need to go. Now."

Sara's phone rang a third time. This time she answered rudely, then said,"So what's new!" She turned to me. "Ray can't drive."

"That's OK," I said, "I will." I quickly canceled a couple of appointments and left with the kids.

Later Jennifer called and told me that Joe had fallen off a ladder and had a concussion. He was not sure anything was wrong until he had tests, so he told Jennifer to keep quiet about it. She felt embarrassed about being late once again and hurt by Sara's "what's new."

Her spirit was flattened by one comment. On the other hand, one small kind word can make a difference.

Several years ago a secretary I worked with was having a terrible day. She was very capable, but it was a busy time of the year. She was on and off the phone, taking care of a huge mailing, and was being interrupted often. She was under a great deal of pressure and had many distractions, and lo and behold, she made a mistake. Now I've worked in several other settings, a hospital, schools, and restaurants. But there is something about a mistake made out of the office of a church that can seem irredeemable to some. Diane dealt with the criticism quite nicely and then turned to me and asked, "Do you remember when you were a little kid and colored a nice picture or picked up your toys, and your mother said to you, 'Aren't you a good girl?'"

"Yeah," I said.

"Well, I know it's not politically correct," she said. "But sometimes I just want to hear someone say, 'You are such a good girl!' It just makes you feel so warm inside."

We laughed, but from time to time after that we told one another, "You are such a good girl!"

The word compassion means "to suffer with." When we see someone suffering pain, humiliation, distress, or isolation we respond with care. We are capable of doing this when we see other people as a mirror of our own humanity. In another person's suffering, mistakes or vulnerability, we can see ourselves, be in solidarity with her, and find ourselves able to act on her behalf. Sometimes the grounds of our meeting are simply common experiences of life and loss.

We know as human beings what it is to be hungry, thirsty, and tired. We have all lost loved ones. So we think of how we have felt and we willingly bring relief or aid or solace. Sometimes we bring comfort even at considerable expense to ourselves. This is what it is to be "little Christs," Martin Luther's words for people who are called into compassion.

We are able to see ourselves in the hurts and problems of others as long as we know that it is permissible and forgivable to be human. And therein lies the rub. The times we have the most trouble acting upon another person's suffering, and the times we are judgmental, are the times we feel most at risk and most afraid to look at ourselves. Like Sara, sometimes we are afraid someone will make us look bad to others. Often the person towards whom we are most judgmental is the person who has characteristics we dislike in ourselves.

A woman, Pam, from a remote rural area, came in to talk to me one day. She told me about finishing graduate work in pharmacy and going out for her first job. She knew about the need for qualified people in health care in rural areas. She had grown up in a small town and it was her dream to go back to the countryside near the place her family still lived, buy a small farm and work where she was really needed.

She started work at a regional hospital but soon was discouraged and very lonely. She was busy and did not get to see her family as often as she liked. Then she discovered that a group of pharmacists in her area met regularly with physicians and others. She went to the meeting with great anticipation. She had the latest information, had graduated with honors from a prestigious university, and was excited at the opportunity to let everyone know who she was and what she had to offer.

The group that gathered there around a coffeepot and a tray of sweet rolls was disappointingly small, and three of the people there were obviously retired. The convener invited everyone to have a seat. There was a short presentation by a speaker and conversation. One of the retirees, Glen, dominated the discussion. Every time someone made a comment he had a response. And his responses were remarkably long. She went away from the meeting disliking him cordially and snubbing him afterward. Glen was only interested in himself, she thought. No one had expressed any interest in her. She was even more discouraged and lonely than when she first went.

When she told me the story, I wondered with her about Glen's motives and his experience. She thought he was probably lonely and that he doubted whether anyone thought he knew anything. As we talked she realized that he did to the group what she had planned to do, and that it was no wonder no one had taken interest in her. She had no interest in them. She discovered compassion for Glen and the rest. She went back to the meetings, and soon had colleagues who respected her and looked forward to seeing her. She discovered compassion for them but first had to admit her own sense of isolation and fear of rejection.

Sometimes we think we are being compassionate but we are just being patronizing. Unless we find what is common between us and accept it, we cannot be truly compassionate. Sometimes we tell ourselves that we know more, or are better off to some degree, or are smarter or genetically superior than someone who is suffering. It helps us put a safe distance between us if we can find a reason for their suffering. If the suffering person is different from us perhaps we can avoid the misery that has befallen her. So we indulge in a great deal of self-deception. Unless we are looking eye to eye with someone in need, we are looking down on him. Then our efforts to help are naturally felt by the recipient as patronizing. We naturally avoid the call to be compassionate to others if we are afraid of their suffering.

We have a natural capacity for compassion because we are born into the human community, and we can imagine people's hurts because we have often endured something similar. We develop even closer ties with many around our common interests, our passions. The passions of so many of those I meet are expressed in their work places and in their family lives. Whether art or sports or music, in every community we create some of this common ground of compassion together. And where we meet over common interests I have observed care for others blossom.

A friend played league softball for years on the same team. An affable, lovable man, he has had diabetes from the time he was a teenager. His wife and kids know the signs of insulin reaction in him. When his blood sugar is low he suddenly gets belligerent, swearing and striking out at loved ones. His family has a stash of candy bars for just such an occasion. He had never told his friends about this because it was so embarrassing.

One day during a tournament, a game went on too long, the schedule was bumped back and his team had no time for lunch. Bud's blood sugar dipped dangerously low. He turned to a teammate and took a swipe at him unprovoked. The man, shorter but bigger than Bud, spun him around and clasped heavy arms around him in a bear hug and they sat on the ground, Bud struggling in his lap. His family ran to him and urged him to eat something, and in a few minutes he was fine." Bud was embarrassed, but his friend waved it off. "I didn't know what was wrong with you," his friend reported. "But it didn't matter. I had to take care of you."

People's passions for many things draw them together. Everywhere I move I learn to create something in a new medium because people in my congregations and communities have unique gifts. As I join them in their lives I learn something from them and we create bonds between us. In Hannaford I learned quilting, Ukrainian egg painting, gardening and about finishing wood. In Grand Forks I learned the art of cooking and entertaining. In Minneapolis I learned to make Danish paper hearts and flat plane Scandinavian woodcarvings. I was taught that it was possible to create something together and that enjoying it was enough. My honest appreciation of their passion for art drew us closer. As we sat working at a table or in a work shed or over a quilting frame, in groups, or two by two, the stories have poured out.

One woman told me about how her house was broken into the summer before. She was mowing the lawn in the front of her house, and a man walked right in the back door, stole her purse and vandalized her house in minutes. This prompted the other women in the group, bent over their stitching, to ask more about her experience, to offer stories about themselves and people they knew who had similar things happen to them. They expressed outrage and compassion for her sense of violation.

Another day a man told me for the first time about the death of his son many years before. He had no brothers, his father died when he was young, and then he lost his son. He told about his profound sorrow. As I expressed concern, another in the group said her son, too, had been killed years ago, and she understood his continued pain and wondering. She, too, was trying to make sense of her loss. A passing motorist was a witness and she heard the story the next day. Her son drove his pickup in the ditch in order to avoid a deer. He knocked over a utility pole, which fell on his car, and he died when he stepped out of his vehicle. He was nineteen. Sympathy poured from those present. But more than that, the compassion of the listeners gave the stories validity and strength. Their sorrow meant something important to others.

A boy casually stopping by and watching a group of us paint heard the sensitive responses of adults to wounds, slights and pain, and began to tell about school. Kids were accosting him nearly every day when he came into the school, dragging him into a restroom near the entrance of the building and pushing him into a toilet. No one knew. Compassion sprouted legs and an irate group called the principal. That day justice was done.

Another day a woman confessed that her daughter, a prominent attorney, murdered several years before, was gay. The group sitting there knew she had been killed, but had never heard the story. "They said they knew she was killed because she was gay because of how it was done," she said, "and because of other things there." Her daughter had been stabbed multiple times; there was blood all over her house as she had fled her attacker. The person who committed the crime left pornographic pictures taped and scattered in various places. The police had never found the killer. They told her it was probably a lover, but Donna knew that was not true. "Any moron would know by what was left there that it wasn't her lover," she spat out. The stunned church quilting group stopped their work, made coffee, and the women held Donna, wishing aloud that they had only known.

Of course, many of the stories were funny, too. A flustered teacher told about one of the kids in her classroom. He was wiggling and wiggling in his seat.

"Ron, do you have to use the restroom?" He shook his head and seriously went to work. Soon he began wiggling again.

"What's the problem, Ron? Can you tell me?" He looked up guiltily, and then shook his head and went back to work. Then he slid over the edge of his seat.

"Ron, stand up, would you?" He put down his pencil and stood up. He bent over slightly.

"Come here." Then she noticed that his pocket was bulging out to the side. "What's in there?"

"Nothing," he replied.

"Empty it," she commanded. He took out an eraser, a paper clip and a piece of bubble gum and put them on her desk. His pocket still stood out.

"Keep going." He bent his knees and took out a wadded up piece of paper and a matchbook.

"You're not supposed to have that here," she scolded him as she took it. He nodded and started to turn, still slouching in an odd way.

"Wait a minute. What else?" Finally, reluctantly, he pulled out a sock, which began to jump. He had found a frog over recess. Knowing Ron, we all roared, in appreciation of his effort, and with understanding for his teacher.

Another woman told the story of driving many miles out into the country with her husband. The car was making a strange noise, a soft, high-pitched noise that they could hear only when they slowed at a stop sign. He wondered if it was the transmission. They drove slowly, then quickly, the husband listening carefully, then punching the accelerator. Finally, thinking a belt was loose and not wanting the car to overheat, he stopped and put up the hood. A flash of fur streaked into the ditch and out into the open field. It was one of their cats.

We gather around common passions, such as sports or art. But we also gather as groups because of suffering. Grief and loss groups, AA meetings, weight loss groups, and therapy groups all have in common a shared experience. Because the members of the group understand one another as others often cannot, their shared experience and acceptance of one another can promote compassion and support for others. Until we can look at ourselves with kindness, we cannot even join such groups and we cannot be compassionate with others in similar situations.

Eve was in and out of the hospital for two years and was very savvy about hospital ways. She was young and vivacious, with dark red curly hair, freckles and brilliant blue eyes. She wore her own expensive looking pajamas and insisted on wearing makeup, even on days when she felt terrible. The large number of visitors to her included her friends and acquaintances who were professionals, politicians or in business. But the hospital staff never saw her husband, Carter. I began to ask her about him. "He's a business entrepreneur," she explained. "He buys businesses and sort of fixes them up. He needs to just do what he's doing." When I asked if she felt bad about that, she looked at me and said, "Oh, Mary, he needs to do that." Another day, when she felt especially awful, I asked where he was. "He's putting in new kitchen carpet." "By himself?" "Uh-huh." I secretly wondered why he was doing that when she seemed to need him and they obviously could afford to have someone else put it in. I asked if she'd like me to call him. "Oh no, Mary, he needs to do that."

Eve did not improve. She was nauseous much of the time. Her friends stopped coming. Nursing staff was increasingly angry with Carter, asking me what was going on. They were only given the number for his secretary, who would find him and tell him any news. "What's Carter up to?" I asked one day. "He's painting." "Painting? Don't you wish he was here?" "Oh, Mary, he needs to do that. He wants the house to be nice." Another day it was landscaping. Another day he was taking care of her car. Finally, one day when I stopped by, she said she was terribly lonely. She talked about their life; how much she and Carter depended on one another, how they were still so much in love. Their families were not close to them and they had decided not to have kids long ago. But she had a dog, Tootsie, a little poodle that was always with her. I asked what would help her that day. She said she wished Tootsie were with her.

So I went to work. I spent a couple of hours finding the hospital policy on pet visitation and how it could work. I talked at length with the charge nurse and that area's supervisor. Two busy physicians had to sign off on it. They were difficult to locate that day and put certain restrictions on the visit. I called Carter's secretary. She was just delighted to hear that Tootsie was being welcomed for a visit and would tell Carter. He would bring the dog around seven that night.

The next day I was eager to hear from Eve about the visit. She was animated in describing how Carter had brought Tootsie and how she had brightened her day. Then she leaned toward me and whispered. "Can you keep a secret?" "Of course," I said. Her eyes twinkled. "Carter has been bringing Tootsie every night." "He comes late at night when there aren't so many people around and hides her under his coat." I burst out laughing as I thought of how the staff was frustrated with him for never visiting and how I had wondered if they even got along well. She reached out and touched my arm. "But it was very nice of you to arrange for Tootsie to come," she gushed.

She knew him so well. "Oh Mary, he needs to do that," I thought. He was getting the house ready for her to come home and doing the work himself. Carter was a doer. In the face of a crisis, he found something to do for Eve. If he couldn't help her in the hospital, then he would make their home as nice as possible. He would do it himself, with his own hands. That Carter did not know what to do was a crisis. He solved his problem the best way he could: he did something. And Eve's compassion for him called me into compassion, too.

The challenge in having true compassion for others is finding common ground and the ability to look at ourselves with compassion. When I am invited to speak for groups who have lesbian or gay children or who want to reach out, I tell my story. There are so many experiences that families and friends of lesbian, gay, bisexual and transgender persons share. The shock of discovery that a child or friend is different than they thought. The initial fears for their safety and their jobs. Guilt about their responses. Worries that their loved one will not be happy. They see that they are in good company, that they are not somehow at fault, that their experience is quite common. They hear from one another that God cares about them and their loved one, that God's declaration in Genesis that creation is good holds true for them. Then the shared experience of having a gay child, family member, or friend gives them a great capacity to care for one another, and more compassion for their loved one.

Even when I speak to a group that I expect to be less friendly or tolerant, I tell my story. There are many common threads between those of us who happen to be gay, and any other human being. In those threads is the basis for us to find compassion for one another. One of the great fears of outsiders to this experience is that there is a homosexual agenda or lifestyle. So I enjoy telling about my lifestyle and my agenda.

My lifestyle is this: I am a sister, aunt, daughter, friend, spouse and mother. I live in a large old stucco house on a block with twenty other old houses. I get up early and walk the dog with Jane, my life partner. We usually talk over our day as we walk. After breakfast and reading part of the paper, I drive my daughter to school and then go on to work. Sometimes I am at work until 9:00 or later at night. When I am lucky, Jane and Hannah and I have dinner together. Sometimes there are bills to pay, a small house repair to be made, homework to do, groceries or other items to buy. I try to go to bed by 10:00, because the morning comes early, as my dad used to say.

My current agenda is to be in the home of at least one parishioner every week, to care for them and my family and the world as best I can, to do some writing every week, to regularly converse with and email my mother, and to have people over for dinner every month. Sometimes things get in the way of my agenda. Then, like everyone else, I can feel very irritable or anxious.

Actually, I think my lifestyle and agenda are much like those of other people. I'm middle class, grew up in a rural area, and am a loyal member of a Protestant church. I vote, am generous within my means to my congregation, and campaigned in my neighborhood for the American Cancer Society and the American Heart Association. I drive a car, take vacations and see relatives during holidays. I have a son in college and a daughter in high school. I watch football and baseball games, enjoy theater and our local symphony orchestra. I have had many other experiences that are like those of other people.

I usually speak to groups of people who are much, much more like me than unlike me. We have a great deal of shared experience in which to find room for one another. I am called into compassion even for those who do not like me at all, because in them I can see myself. I have unfairly judged others. I have had trouble relating to people who were different from me, and I have missed some people entirely. I have caused suffering to countless people in ways small and great, knowingly and unknowingly, and sometimes even felt justified in doing so.

Aware or not, our experiences continually call us into compassion in our daily life. I was standing out in my yard with a young carpenter, looking at my roof and the down spouts and trying to figure out where a wall air conditioner should be placed. A van pulled up along the curb. Tom, the contractor for many projects on my old house, stepped out and joined us. He was a little late, but I didn't think too much about it. He's a busy person.

He greeted us cheerfully and I asked how he was doing. He said, "It's been quite a morning." I asked what had been happening. He always has some amusing story, so I expected him to tell about one of the people he worked for. He started to tell about the garden he was just breaking in someone's yard and described it for a minute. Then he finally said, "And I started out the day behind, because we got a call at three-thirty in the morning to go over to my mother-in-law's house. My father-in-law passed away suddenly."

"Oh no, Tom, I'm so sorry."

"It was a big surprise," he said, and began to describe the scene. Relatives were already there sitting on the couch and his mother-in-law was sobbing. The rescue squad and the police came. They had to wait several hours for the coroner to pronounce him dead because he died at home unexpectedly. Meanwhile, the body of his father-in-law lay there. Since it was a small apartment, whenever one wanted to go from one room to the other, one had to step over him.

Tom told the story with a lot of humor and drama. But it was obvious how traumatic it must have been, and even though Tom handled it with his usual aplomb and humor, my heart was breaking for him. In the middle of his story I reached up and gave him a big hug. He burst into tears and began to tell how really difficult and overwhelming it was for him.

We are called into compassion as we realize that the people with whom we work and live are much like us. We share a great deal of our humanity. We become intimates in matters of our hearts, our passions, our love for work or life, our difficulties and our disappointments. When people know that we accept them however they come and feel compassion for them, a level of trust develops that is unlike anything else. We can trust them with our work and life, and they can trust us with their sorrows and their hopes and dreams. We do not need to hide.

Sermon • March 21, 2003

> *"But we had to celebrate and rejoice, because this brother of yours was dead and has come to life; he was lost and has been found."* (Luke15:32)

I don't know about you, but I want to know what happens next in this story of the Prodigal. The son comes home from living with pigs, is welcomed into a running father's arms, and all is watched by a glowering, jealous older son, who, the father says, can have everything. Now that the father has given him everything, what will he do? What more will he want?

The story is so familiar. Let me tell it to you a little different way. Once there were two rather spoiled young women. They lived with their mother, who owned a prosperous grocery store. The older daughter was helpful, responsible and careful. Maybe just a bit overbearing. Maybe even a tad boring. But she was with her mother, understood the business' details, worked long hours, went to college and got an accounting degree and did the taxes.

The younger daughter was never too much invested in the whole scene. She took it for granted, all her mother's hard work and years of careful investing and shrewd business decisions. She thought the place was a bit garish. She was sometimes a little embarrassed of her mom. She wore the same old brown suit all the time and was proud of it. The younger daughter was often tired from her nights out, so she avoided work as much as possible. And when she graduated from high school, she marched into her mom's office and told her wanted her share of the inheritance. Well, there was an argument. Mom wouldn't pay for college later when she'd blown it all. If she took her money now, she wouldn't give her half, but only a third. Yes, yes . . . she said. She'd been getting her way all her life. Today was no different. As her older sister sat there dumbfounded, good old mom took out her checkbook and wrote out a check for one-third of her worth. Then her younger daughter, true to form, took off.

The younger daughter traveled for a couple of years—Morocco, Japan, Australia, wherever she felt like. She took friends with her. Paid their way. After all, it'd be boring, wouldn't it, to go alone? She bought them extravagant gifts. When there was almost nothing left, she landed in L.A. and she found an investor. With him she deposited the rest of her money. He promised huge interest rates. She thought she was quite smart, smarter than mom who eked out her living with hard work. She figured that within a couple of years she would have much of her money back. Maybe she'd go back and show off her new car, her jewelry, try to get her boring sister to do something, anything.

But you all know what happened. The investor was a crook, stock prices went bust and she lost everything. She was attractive, so she tried to make it as an actress, and before she really knew what was happening, she found herself living in her uninsured car, working in a restaurant, and eating food off the plates when her manager wasn't looking. Some nights she was so hungry, she waited until everyone went home and rescued what she could from the dumpster. But then one night she came to herself. She remembered her home, the food there, her mother's kindness. She thought surely her mother would at least hire her as a cashier. So she stole money from the till, filled her car with gas and headed for home.

It was early Sunday morning when she turned her car into her mother's driveway in Edina, Minneasota. Her mother was in her bathrobe, reading the paper. When she saw her youngest standing there at the door, she was wildly happy. "Can I stay?" "But of course!"

And as the daughter got some things from the car her mother ran barefoot in her robe out into the yard, jumping up and down and yelling, "Woo hoo!! I'm going to empty the shelves of the store, and have a party for the neighborhood. No, the whole town! Whoopee!!!"

The elder sister woke up with the racket, looked out the window and scowled when they came back into the house. It had been a very difficult last three years. The financial hit they had taken when dear little Susie Q left was huge, and now that they were back on their feet through sheer struggle, long, long hours, laying off employees, and complete sacrifice, the ingrate has the nerve to come back. And mother acts like a complete idiot. She will make them poor again. They cannot afford a big party.

So she confronts her. "What is the deal here? She's already had hers. Now she's back. You're such a sucker for her, Mom. What more will she want?"

"But the lost is found," she says. "The dead is alive. Oh, isn't it wonderful we have her back?"

But the older daughter does not think it is wonderful. She is absolutely livid.

So the mother says, "Get my checkbook, dear. All that I have is yours. What more do you want?" And once again, the mother takes up her pen. This time to write a check for the full amount of the value of her business and her house. And she hands it to her older daughter.

So you see. I just want to know what happens next. . . . Now that the mother has impoverished herself, giving first to the one what she never deserved and pouring out everything for the other, what will her daughters do? Because the story isn't finished. The story of the Prodigal. It's never finished.

Now that the mother has impoverished herself, giving first to all the ones who never deserved anything their share of the inheritance, and then welcoming them back when they blow it, then giving to the other one all the rest, everything. Now that the mother has done that, what will the children do?

And the story goes on. . . . You see, it doesn't matter where you see yourself in the story, which daughter or son you identify with, the prodigal who over and over finds himself on the dole with the almighty, or with the responsible one who feels that playing by the rules hasn't really paid off. The point is that the mother has poured herself out for you, has given you everything, has written a check for everything and handed it to you. God is with you the whole time. What more do you want? And what will you do now?

The story goes on and on. . . . And on and on. God writes the checks and we spend them. We like to think that because we follow the rules not only will we be rewarded, but the prodigals won't get a thing. This prodigal son was not nice, that daughter who was willing to take her mother's hard-earned money was not nice. They were manipulative and rude, and we can't be sure that they even really ever changed. And the story goes on. God writes the checks and we spend them. What more do you want? Are you afraid God will not deal justly with you? Fine, the check just comes to you with Jesus crucified on it. What more do you want?

There is a whole world outside these doors, convinced that no one cares about them. Convinced that life is meaningless. Convinced that because they were born the way they were born or made the choices that they have made or had the things happen to them that have happened, that they are unlovable. All those outcasts, those prodigals, those sinners. Like the ones who ate with Jesus. Not one of them needs your judgment or your disdain or your hatred or worse, your apathy. And all those older brothers and sisters—are you afraid to pour God's love out to them? What more do you want? Yet another check from God? What more do you want? Jesus' very life? What more do you want? God's own body and blood? Well, you are welcome to it.

Called into Sorrow

If you knew how it would turn out you would never jump into it. – Elsie, on the death of her husband.

There are many things in life that we do not choose. I have often wondered what my life would have been like had I not grown up in a place where I could walk out the front door and see for miles. To the north of our house and through a little grove of trees my grandmother waited with cookies and uncritical love. Across the driveway and down a lane were farm animals of every kind, which to a child held their own fascinations. To the south we could see several miles, rectangles of different crops and occasional trees and homes. From the backyard of my house we could see the steeple of the small country church to which we belonged, a mile away. Had I not enjoyed these things, my life would have had different roots; it would have begun from a different perspective. I did not choose that beginning.

Nor did I choose many other things. I have five siblings. They simply arrived at their various times and in their own ways. I did not ask for them, nor was there any question about sending them back if I did not approve of them. I am tall, and I had no choice about that. My height was simply given to me. So were my hair color, the size of my feet, my socioeconomic situation, the color of my skin, my parents' occupations and vocations, and my extended relatives. Especially when we are young, the most important pieces of life are gifts, unasked for, unplanned, some pleasant and happy, and others not. We do not choose much of life and the unwanted things can cause us great sorrow.

We like to think we have a great deal of freedom and choice, but in reality we are simply given so many things. Life itself is a gift to us, but the moment we have it, we are vulnerable to losing it and suffering its accompanying sorrow. As soon as we have a child we are afraid someone will drop her. As soon as she can ride a bicycle or drive a car we are afraid she will hurt herself. We risk loving others and immediately upon doing so make ourselves vulnerable to loss. Still, we find grief somehow unexpected, even when we have been prepared for death. We usually don't choose loss. It, too, is a gift, an unwanted one. We are vulnerable in many ways, so we are often called into sorrow.

As I drove into the churchyard for the first funeral over which I officiated, I thought with a great deal of panic that I must be late. I intended to arrive an hour early, but the little church yard that surrounded St. Olaf Lutheran in Walum was packed with cars, more cars than I had ever seen in one place in the community. The church is beautiful, white clapboard with stained glass windows. The graveyard, surrounded with evergreens, frames the back. I ran to the carved wooden door. I could hear music playing. The funeral director was there at the top of red carpeted steps near the entrance to the sanctuary. Embarrassed, I asked him what time the service was to begin. He told me with a laugh that I had an hour. I walked to the sacristy at the front of the sanctuary, which was full of people, save the first rows cordoned off with a thick gold rope for immediate family. Everyone was dressed in their Sunday best, suits and ties, dresses and heels, and sat quietly and expectantly waiting for the service to begin. They understood the importance of funerals, of expressing corporate sorrow, in that little community.

The woman who had died was a resident in a nearby nursing home for many years because of a severe stroke. I visited her in the nursing home several times, but she was unresponsive and the staff didn't know much about her. So I read to her and prayed with her. She had never married and she had no family, so there was no service the night before, and the funeral director was not much help. So we had the funeral, and though she had been in the nursing home for many years, the church was full, as was the custom in those congregations. I preached about her illness and God's restoration of her in the last day. She was in the arms of God.

Just as we were about to do the benediction an elderly woman stood up. "Can I say something?" Without waiting for us to respond, she continued. "She wasn't just a teacher. She promoted programs for young people and was active in her congregation and community. She started a summer camp for kids and she was an advocate for all the children. She didn't have her own, but every child in this town was important to her. They all knew her and loved her. She's gone, but I for one will never forget what she did. I just wanted you to know it." Then she sat down. I was stunned for an instant and then thanked her. There was nothing really wrong with what we did or said. The sermon and service were nice. They just didn't call us into the life of the deceased. We could have tried harder to get more information, even when it wasn't immediately forthcoming.

So the next time it was my turn to be with a family in grief, I asked them for their stories. Those stories, funny and touching, nearly always found their way into sermons for the one who had died. Their stories became the touchstone for the community and a catalyst for more conversation. The stories were always about the gift the person was to the community and each one there and the ways they were called into sorrow because of their loss.

Years later, when a woman who had ALS, a devastating illness, died, those family stories brought people back together who had been estranged for years. Mara's husband, now a recovering alcoholic, had offended many family members and old friends so that they were no longer speaking. Mara defended him, and by the time she contracted her illness, they were nearly totally isolated from the community.

When Mara died they all gathered at a funeral home for the family service. During that time I invited stories. The pain was on everyone's faces. Mara's husband sat in the front row with his head hanging. No one would speak. I waited quietly. Then a few talked about how they loved her and had missed her and how they had felt shut out. Then a son stood up and spoke of his guilt for not overcoming the barriers.

There was a long uncomfortable silence. One friend finally stood. "I don't know if this is appropriate," she began, "but you know Mara was always fixing something." People looked at one another. "One day she told me she was tired of her bedroom rug. It was a crazy idea, but she decided to paint the floor and wanted to know if I'd help." She looked over at me. "She was always roping me into something. I agreed to help her, Lord save me, and went over there. She already had the paint and brushes and we went to work. But Mara hadn't thought it through, so we started at the door and started painting. And I think you know where I'm going with this." Everyone began to giggle. " We didn't realize it but we were painting ourselves into a corner. But that wasn't the worst of it. The bed was in the corner and too heavy to move, so first we painted around it." Now there was loud laughter. "Then we crawled under it with our paint brushes. Mara humped up her back and lifted it and we crawled backwards and painted under it. But we did it! The last time we were over there that floor was still blue."

Others told funny stories about this vigorous and engaging woman. At the end of the service, they mingled and chatted and reached out to one another with many tears. A great healing had occurred as they were called into their sorrow.

There are many things in life that we do not choose. Some are insignificant and some are dramatic. I did not choose to be gay. I can choose what to do with that discovery, but I cannot change the fact of it. For many years I did not want to be called into this sorrow. I had seen enough of it.

Beginning in my twenties I suffered from episodes of depression. When I was forty years old I went into therapy because I was once again in a dark cloud of despair. It made no sense. I had just taken a position in a wonderful congregation. I was excited about the possibilities of ministry. But I desperately missed my friend I had come to know in my previous workplace. I was tired of it all and determined to do whatever it took to be free. I knew that depression is sometimes thought to be suppressed anger or the expression of a loss of faith. I tried to think about what I was angry about and could not come up with anything. I wondered if a person could lose their faith and not know, because I usually felt that my only safe place was my relationship with God. In therapy I came to the amazing and awful realization that I was in love with a woman, and the depressions I had suffered were related to incidents when I was especially in tune with the pain and suffering of gay people.

I was in shock and felt lost, and I was very paranoid. I thought everyone must know. They must be able to see how lost and dismembered and disorganized I was. During that period of time, I was swayed by almost anyone else's opinions about anything. I no longer trusted my own judgment. The questions continually going through my mind were, "How could I have missed that about myself? How could this have happened?" I took several writing assignments and taught on the side in addition to my parish work. I kept a journal. I lost sleep and worked long hours in order to be tired enough to rest. A psychiatrist thought I should be on medication, but when I tried it I felt slow and thick, so I quit taking it. He thought I was ill, but my therapist recommended another psychiatrist who said, "You're not sick, you're just creative. And very sad." Of course, and what a relief that was. I was sad.

Making a decision to not be depressed, ironically, called me into my sorrow. In order to do that, I had to come out. I had to integrate those pieces of myself that I had discovered that were separate from the rest of my life. Everyone around me had to be called into sorrow too. It took us several years to untangle what that meant.

When I came out, when I allowed myself to speak the truth, I was called into tremendous sorrow. The whole landscape of my life changed. I lost my husband, a good and caring person, who was also a bright and faithful colleague. I lost his insight and support, his willingness to work, his encouragement. I lost his entire family, people I had spent every major occasion with for many years. I have especially missed his sister and her family. I lost several friends, some of whom were good friends of Bob, whom he needed during the difficult times of transition. I wrote letters and talked to family members. They were all kind to me, but the relationships we have had changed in some ways. They have been good and gracious, to their credit. Some of my friends have not. One of my dearest friends, shocked that I had not shared details of my situation with her first, told me that she hoped I suffered. All of my relationships changed.

I experienced overwhelming change and loss at work. I left the congregation I was serving before I came out. I did not want a schism there. They had not chosen a lesbian for their staff, nor any of the craziness and complication that any of that could bring. So I began a course of study and gave them some time to have a replacement for me before we told anyone. I stayed away even though several people contacted me and encouraged me to come back. I missed preaching and teaching, and I sorely missed all the people. I visited several congregations and finally settled on one where I could worship. I joined choirs and got to know the pastors there.

I bought a home a mile from my old home, and we divided our things. In the evening, when I came home from work, I fixed and painted my new place. I was exhausted but did not know who to ask for help with anything. I had lost my sense of community. I no longer knew exactly where I belonged. My vocation as a pastor was behind me, I was sure, as well as my writing and teaching and any standing in my religious community. I loved the church and felt it was taken away in a fundamental way.

Of course, for all that I lost, my husband, children, family, congregation, friends, and neighbors also were called into sorrow. Sorrow for them and for all of us together. The stories of nearly all the gay people I talk to, but especially religious gay people, have a strong element of being called into sorrow. Without taking that frightening step, and without experiencing the loss, there is no life. The more we love, the more we risk. We are called into sorrow.

But as soon as the psychiatrist put a name on it, as painful as it was, I knew what to do. Though it was not easy, I had been called into sorrow many times before. There are many things in life that we do not choose. Divorce, job changes and losses, and moving are difficult when we choose them, and even worse when others choose them and they affect us. Our neighbor's divorce, for example, can take away our child's playmate and our friend and give us someone for whom we did not ask. Our spouse or parent or child can abandon us. We are often called into sorrow.

One Holy Week in Hannaford, as a spiritual discipline, I decided to make a quilt. It was something women in that community could understand completely, how I could wish to do so even though I was very busy, and especially so when I was serving in five congregations. During every spare moment I chose a pattern and then cut apart old left over pieces of material. After I'd pieced the top of the quilt together, I went to Elsie with it for her help. We went to a fabric store, and she helped me choose a border and gave me instructions for sewing it all together. Then we put in on her quilting frame, along with a beautiful plain back and batting, and the two of us sat together in her front room many hours and quilted it. She stitched her name in one corner. I use that quilt half the year.

I'm not sure why I chose that time to make a quilt. But we buried a lot of kids in Hannaford that year. They weren't all members of our congregations, but we were a resource in a place where there weren't that many clergy. We were close to the age of many of those young parents, and perhaps they thought we could better understand. I suppose that was part of it. We would sit and listen even if we couldn't really comprehend the extent of their losses. And they were gracious enough to share them.

One gray morning we got a call. A car had rolled over the night before. The driver had hit loose gravel. It was only ten o'clock at night. Four teenagers were in the car. One was thrown out as the car tumbled through the ditch and was killed. She was sixteen and strikingly beautiful. Her father gave her long, dark hair and courage. Her mother gave her a quiet, sensitive nature. Bob went to the farm that morning. He came home to say the small house a few miles in the country was so full that one could not squeeze in the door. He stood in the yard that now looked like a county fair parking lot and talked with people as they came and went. The family belonged to an Assemblies of God church, and in their small congregation, death was celebrated in a narrow way as an event for which God is to be praised. No claims were made for the girl's salvation, though they hoped fervently that she was saved. In their little congregation, sadness was not expressed. It was a sign of faithlessness.

That night I received a whispered phone call. It was the girl's mother. Could I come right away? I went out to the farm. The door was open to the house. Family and friends were sitting around the kitchen and living room. I expressed my condolences. They corrected me and praised God. I didn't know them, and left a short time later, wondering about the purpose of the phone call.

As I walked down the concrete back steps, the girl's mother caught me by the arm. "Could you stay for a minute?" "Sure," I said turning to go back inside. "No, not in there," she said quickly. "How about right here?" We sat on the narrow steps and she took a deep breath. "It's been terrible and I feel sinful because I am so sad." I made a sound of sympathy, and she turned to me, held out her arms and began to sob. I simply held her. I told her even Jesus wept. After a long time she collected herself, looked guiltily at the door, thanked me and told me she'd better go. I still don't know exactly why she called me, of all the people in her community. I couldn't recall having even met her before. But when her daughter's funeral was held at the school gym, she asked me to read the letters from her daughter's schoolmates.

We were called into sorrow. In part, Suzanne, taught us. In similar circumstances a few years before we took our call there, Suzanne's son Johnny had been killed when his new pickup truck hit a soft patch of gravel, caught the hard border of grass along the edge and rolled off the road. He was thrown out of the truck and crushed as it rolled over him. Four years later, people still talked about it as if it had happened the previous day. In a town of 200 everybody knows everybody and is even related in some way to most. Everybody knew Johnny, and within an hour after the crash every person in Hannaford knew what had happened. Within a few days most people in the county would know. We were told the story when we asked about the house across the street. We didn't see people come and go much. Suzanne and her daughter lived there but kept pretty much to themselves after the accident. It was a part of the shock wave of devastation the town experienced when they lost Johnny.

As young pastors, we eventually heard the story about Johnny from the previous pastor and wondered how we would deal with the funeral of a beloved child. We had no idea that in this small community four children would die in the next two years.

The first year, a young boy accidentally hanged himself one evening while playing a Halloween trick on his sister. The two volunteer Emergency Medical Technicians who arrived were teachers who once had him in their classes, but they were too late to save him. Once again, the entire town was devastated. The boy's family lived in a small home and the next day casseroles, bread, sandwiches, cookies and salads began to arrive. The refrigerator upstairs and the freezer downstairs were filled. On every horizontal surface either food lay waiting or a family member perched.

People came to pay their respects. The house was crammed full of people. Kids were shooed to make room for the pastors. The boy's father leaned against a kitchen counter, red-eyed and hoarse from telling the details of the story. The legend was forming; the family added some new thoughts, molding their tale of grief. Over and over he told of the rolling tipped chair, the rope not even tied, the little sister afraid and quiet. The story would be repeated all around town, at the post office, the grocery store, the bowling alley and café. Tears would be spent, sympathy expressed for the boy, his parents, his brothers and sisters, the teachers, the boy's five classmates.

As we were leaving someone was coming in the door. The conversation hushed; the house grew quiet. Everyone had seen her come. It was Suzanne. The boy's mother was near the door and she hugged Suzanne like she never intended to let go. Suzanne held her up as she sobbed. And all Suzanne said was, "I know, I know." These were words that hardly anyone there could say, "I know." We would see this scenario acted out again. The news of a young one's death, the futile trip to the hospital, the house filled with mourners and food, time stopping as Suzanne came into the house and embraced the newly grieving with the arms of God.

Eventually we gained the same talent, the weight of the many we served who died. Each time, my heart was very heavy, and in the beginning I wondered how pastors who had lived with the people and genuinely loved them could stand it. Eventually I came to appreciate the capacity of the heart and that the only way to bear the great weight of the sorrow of so many is to enter it as oneself and embrace it as a sign of the richness of life. I was called into sorrow.

In Hannaford I learned that it was often enough to show up. I had enough good sense to understand that I couldn't do a thing except help them listen to themselves, remind them that God cared for them and that they were capable of surviving, and help them find the courage to again put one foot in front of the other. Car accidents. A murder. An accidental hanging. Electrocution. Cancer. Heart failure. Stroke. Each captured a lovely person and took them away from us within a short span of time.

Our hearts broke with the families as each one died. The children were especially traumatic for us all. We suffered through what was lost—a young life with so much ahead, hopes and dreams. And so during that busy Holy Week, Elsie and I made a lovely quilt. Our quilt was a concrete way of putting together pieces of grief that honored the community and our call into sorrow together.

Evan was sitting up in his hospital bed in a navy blue monogrammed bathrobe and matching slippers with pillows fluffed behind him. Half glasses sat at the end of his nose as he read a newspaper. A cell phone lay in his lap and when it rang he answered in a sentence or two and was done. When a nursing aide came in, he politely asked for ice water. But it was not so much a request as an order. His well-manicured wife sat nervously in the windowsill, chatting with him and simultaneously digging in her large bag. Most people who come into the hospital are feeling so ill or out of place and so nervous that they are lying down. Evan was in charge from the beginning. I conversed with him for a short time, discovered that he was Roman Catholic and that he wanted a priest to come. He said he felt okay, but was in for a few days for chemotherapy. It was interrupting the business he owned. I offered to return to talk, he simply waved his hand in a friendly way. But we were done.

He was back a couple of weeks later because of pain. This time we had a longer talk because I was part of a pain team, physicians, nurse, and pharmacists, who were referred to patients struggling with extreme or unremitting pain. He talked about how his illness was taking away his sense of control. He expected to go home the next day, but two weeks later he was still there. Now the bathrobe was nowhere to be seen, nor was the veneer of calm or respectfulness to others. The next day, at the request of staff, who were grappling with his anger, I went in to see him. He was struggling to telephone his wife. I helped him make the call. "Where is she?" he wondered as I dialed. "She never shows up," he complained. He was unable to reach her, but a few minutes later she walked in the door, kindly explaining she had been taking care of errands he had requested. He angrily told her that as a wife she ought to be with him, that he needed her now and she could no longer just ignore him. She shrugged her shoulders and changed the subject.

Later that day as I passed near his room his nurse caught me once again. Would I see Evan again? He was calling everyone who came into his room liars, and he wanted to talk to me. I went into his room and he was perched on the edge of his bed, his feet dangling. "Come here, would you?" he demanded. I sat in a chair next to him. "You're a pastor and can't lie, right?"

"I certainly try not to," I said, wondering where he was going.

"OK, then. Everybody around here is lying to me." At that moment his wife walked in. "They are talking about me behind my back and I know they are lying about me." He turned to his wife. "And you too!"

"I heard that you were upset about that," I said.

"But you're a religious person and won't lie, right?"

"Right."

"Answer me this: Am I dying?"

His wife grabbed his hand. "Evan, don't do this again."

I looked him straight in the eyes and said, "I don't know. But I can find someone who can tell you that."

"Thank you," he said.

One of the hardest tasks for physicians, particularly oncologists, is telling patients how long they will live. After all, they are not God, and they have dedicated their lives to healing. So they estimate to the best of their ability when asked, and still hope for the best for their patients. And I understood what was going on for those around Evan. They didn't want him to give up, and to them he wasn't dying. Not in the next few days. But Evan was a planner, an organizer, who needed to be in charge, even of his death. I found an oncologist outside the door of Evan's room. I repeated the conversation I had just had and he came into the room with me and told him that a lot of people at his stage live for two years.

So I turned to the doctor and asked, "But will this disease kill him?"

"Eventually it will. Yes," the doctor said in a kindly way.

Evan sat up and said triumphantly, "I thought so." The doctor left.

"Please, Evan, let's not talk about this," his wife pleaded, still holding his hand.

"Why did you want to hear about this, Evan?" I asked. "Are you making plans?"

"Yes," he said. "We need a wheel chair ramp at the back of the house, and if I just say the word Chet will have one on there tomorrow. How else will I be able to get around anymore at home?" And he went on to talk about other practical issues about their home.

We listened for awhile and then I turned to his wife. "And why did you not want him to talk about this?" A barrier between them cracked with her cheerful façade and then tumbled down as she burst into tears. "Because I can't bear the thought of losing him."

He reached for her and she climbed beside him on the bed and he comforted her as she wept. They came out to one another about their fear and loss and in doing so were able to comfort one another.

I got a call from Eve's nurse. She was actively dying, Carter was there, would I come quickly. I met the elusive Carter, the dog smuggler, for the first time. He was standing next to Eve, but came to the door when I arrived. "Well, there's nothing to do here," he said, after I looked at her for a moment, held her hand and greeted her. "Is there anyplace around here where I can buy you a cup of coffee and we can sit and talk? This is too depressing."

I looked at Eve and wondered about leaving her. Knowing she might be able to hear, I told her we'd be back soon. We are never prepared fully for sorrow. Those who have loved wholeheartedly know that best.

Comfort, comfort my people, says your God. Speak tenderly and cry to her that she has served her term. But what shall I cry out? We are like grass that withers. It is the Lord who is constant (Isaiah 40:1-2, 6-8). So says the prophet Isaiah. We are in the end utterly vulnerable and obliged to others. We are called into sorrow. That is what it is to be human. God's response to us is compassion. We are broken and dismembered from our communities. God remembers and draws us into a larger story. We are filled with false pride and judgment of others. God is righteous. The world is far from perfect, and yet we can live into it with trust and hope, knowing there is a future for us where righteousness will be at home. We are called into sorrow and God is there with us. Between dismemberment and

God's remembering. Between the imperfect present and the new heavens and new earth. I understand more about the incarnation, God in human form, after working with people who are called into sorrow. God comes as close as our lips, as close as our skin, as close as our breath, only in the body of another. We have God's word in print, the stories of how God's journey is intertwined with ours. We have the majesty of the material world, awe-inspiring landscapes. We have the comfort of music, the soaring cadences of Bach. We have our precious liturgies and services of prayer and praise. But God's love is only really accessible in the love and care of one another, like in the love between Eve and Carter. I heard Eve's voice who knew Carter best. "Oh, Mary, he needs to do that." So we got coffee.

Carter had no one else except an estranged brother. He didn't even know where he lived. His heart was broken. What would he do next? Could we walk and talk? Sure. So we walked outside until we got cold and then around and around the gymnasium at the hospital. Carter was a mover and shaker. He was used to getting things done. But he didn't know how to do a funeral. Eve was a good person. She should have a good funeral. But who would come if they didn't have a family? And who would speak, and who would sit beside him? We talked about his pain and the darkness. We talked about his church and his pastor. And we talked about why we do Christian funerals, to mourn and celebrate the life of the person and shake a fist at death, not letting it have the last word on our lives. Then we went back to Eve. He kissed her awkwardly, thanked her, and said, "See you later, kid." and left in tears. I went to Eve and held her hand, so she wouldn't die alone. Her body was so small that the sheet was barely disturbed. She was a husk of what she had been. As I looked down at her I thought she could have been eighty, rather than thirty-five.

I remembered my Grandmother on her deathbed. Her health had been failing for some time. She had trouble walking. Her vision was impaired. She enjoyed so few things because she could no longer sit through church or dinner in a restaurant or a meeting. I had an old Volkswagen Bug and would help her out to it. She would grasp the handle on the dash in front of her with both hands and put her face close to the windshield and laugh aloud. She called the car the Bubble. We went places she hadn't seen in years. A little lake near her home, hardly bigger than a pond, called Timber Lake, had a little parking area close to its shore. We had a little outing there one day at sunset and it was as though we'd driven to the Atlantic. She exclaimed over the water and sky and on her deathbed, when she was hardly a bump under the covers, she asked, "How is the Bubble?" I thought of her as I stood near Eve.

Eve's face lay sideways, her eyes closed, all her lovely red hair gone, her hands, laying on top of the sheets, dotted with large, rosy bruises. A tube came from her side. I saw Christ before me, incarnate, in her gentle face, in the wounds on her hands and in her side, and in the gentle and flawed love between two. And in that holy moment I recognized God's compassion. Not because events turn out well and happy, but because I recognized in the love of two a small reflection of God's care. I was filled with hope for all of us. We are loved and have been promised a future where this grace is not such a fleeting thing. Meanwhile, we are called into sorrow and God is with us. Not any God, but the one made flesh, who knows with compassion our suffering, our humiliations small and great, and our tender and inadequate love for one another, which is finally our clearest harbinger of that hope.

We do not happily say our farewells. But I have watched the agony of death transformed many times as the

Spirit of God redeemed those moments. We are reminded over and over again that we are sojourners only in this life. We stay in one place and then another. We age. We move on. We touch one another and in an instant we are separated. We need one another and lose one another in a breathtaking fashion. We are called into sorrow many times over. Sometimes we are called into a ministry of leaving and being left. Sometimes that calling allows us to know when to let go so that life can begin again.

Sermon • All Saints

> *After this I looked, and there was a great multitude that no one could count, from every nation, from all tribes and peoples and languages, standing before the throne and before the Lamb, robed in white, with palm branches in their hands. Then one of the elders addressed me, saying, "Who are these, robed in white, and where have they come from?" I said to him, "Sir, you are the one that knows." Then he said to me, "These are they who have come out of the great ordeal; they have washed their robes and made them white in the blood of the Lamb. For this reason they are before the throne of God, and worship him day and night within his temple, and the one who is seated on the throne will shelter them. They will hunger no more, and thirst no more; the sun will not strike them, nor any scorching heat; for the Lamb at the center of the throne will be their shepherd, and he will guide them to springs of the water of life, and God will wipe away every tear from their eyes."* (Rev 7:9,13-17 NRSV).

I always think of my uncle on All Saints Day. I'm not sure of all the reasons. But one is that when he died several years ago, he taught me how a funeral ought to be done. My uncle Herb requested "Joyful, Joyful We Adore Thee" for his funeral, and as we sang it, I was struck by what I thought was the incongruity of a hymn of praise at such an event, and also the gift that hymn was to us. So whenever I hear that hymn and when I reflect on All Saints, I think of him.

He was a typical Norwegian American farmer, with huge hands, a gruff manner, a wonderful baritone voice and a great dry sense of humor. He and my aunt produced only two sturdy, strong sons, my cousins. A daughter died at birth. And so he came to love his nieces, who were boisterous and impetuous, as though they were his own. He loved me and loved my sisters. He was simply there and taken for granted in a friendly way, in a way that only family can be—at family celebrations, at church every Sunday, during harvest on our farm, on lazy Sunday afternoons. And he looked just like my father, though a few years older. To look on him in his casket was to have my breath stolen away because it was like living a moment in the future.

And because of that glimpse of the future, and because of the joyful gift of a hymn of praise as we paid our final tribute and gave him into the arms of Jesus, with Uncle Herb's funeral I fully understood his place and my place and your place in the hymn that speaks of the great host of those who are robed in white at the throne of God.

Who is this host arrayed in white,
Like thousand snowclad mountains bright,
That stands with palms and sing its psalms,
Before the throne of light?
(Copyright 1978, Lutheran Book of Worship)

He's missed so much, that dear uncle of mine. He's missed Dan playing the piano and Hannah losing her teeth. He missed his sons' 25th wedding anniversaries. He missed my preaching debut to the grandstand crowd at the fabulous Jackson County Fair near my hometown. (He would have appreciated my jokes about seed corn.) He's missed knowing all our accomplishments great and small, and all our sadnesses. He's missed the seasonal rhythm of family life. And we have missed him too.

Who is this host arrayed in white that stand around the throne? My Uncle Herb is there with all the saints of God. He's there with all the others that we now miss—Bernice, Bertha, Clarence and Anna, Mary and Evelyn, Lars, Lorelei, Daniel, Shirley and Art, and all the friends and family we remember with thankfulness and some sadness this All Saints Day.

And so my thoughts today about All Saints twine around a hymn, a sadness and a word from God about a vision of Jesus among the saints.

Who is this host arrayed in white? In the past Sundays, with warm water carefully set out by loving hands under the glow of the Christ candle, accompanied by words etched into the cornerstone of Christian tradition, several little ones have been baptized into the family of faith in the name of the Triune God. Dressed all in white, in their baptismal best, they became the saints of God.

Who is this host arrayed in white? Last Sunday, sober and nervous lest they make some terrible, life-threatening, embarrassing mistake, Evan and Michael affirmed their baptismal vows that their parents and adult friends had made on their behalves some 15 years ago. Standing there in their white robes, they too were a part of the host of saints.

Who is this host arrayed in white? The hymn tells us.

These are the saints who kept God's Word;
They are the honored of the Lord.

Who is this host arrayed in white? As we journey through our lives in the church, we each in our turn wear the white robes that remind us of our baptism, of God's great creative love, of Jesus' blood and sacrifice for us, of the Holy Spirit's continual witness to God. We are gently reminded time and again of the sainthood of all of us sinners. For at the same time that God looks at us, and sees all the darkness and foolishness and sin, God also sees Jesus.

He is their prince, who drowned their sins,
So they were cleansed, restored.

On this All Saints, I have a vision of the saints and of their savior. It is a picture given to us in the Word. There stands a strong man with rough hands, wood chips clinging to his clothing, and love in his eyes. He was the one who hung on a cross, suffering, dying, and yet with his last breath forgiving and reconciling those beside him and below him to himself and each other, and then reconciling the whole world to God.

And now he is the host at a table—life pouring from his hands into the chalice for us, serving a host of people, young and old, kneeling alongside one another as they sing a song of praise and thanksgiving. Here are Abraham and Sarah, hands lifted to receive God, and here are the Apostle Peter and Paul still arguing about where mission money should be sent. Here too kneel Priscilla and Aquila, who can't believe they are still arguing. Now some Pentecostals come praying and waving their hands in the air and some Danes dancing to the table to be served the body and blood that forgives and reconciles. Next to them are some staid Norwegians who will never dance, but can't help but tap their toes. Here is Bernice smiling at Lorelei who is raising her hands up in the air and dancing as she sings along with them. Here is Lars welcoming all and Evelyn and Art with their arms full of flowers. Here, too, is my uncle with his fine baritone. He's with grandpa and grandma and the baby he never even knew. And here are all your loved ones too, the faithful who have gone before you. They have all joined the song. We kneel next to them, the body of Christ gathered and given. And we join the eternal song of the saints, a hymn of praise.

Who is this host arrayed in white? All the saints of God.
They now serve God both day and night;
They sing their songs in endless light.
Their anthems ring when they all sing.
With angels shining bright.

Called into Love

I loved you before I met you. – Grandma Frederickson reminiscing about my birth.

I received a breathless phone call. Our friend Kristin told me she had just heard from her mother in Denmark about her eighty-year-old grandmother who lived in the same city. Her aorta was infected and she would have surgery in two days. I called people on the prayer chain in my congregation. I received a couple of phone calls with questions about her. The next Sunday morning, we remembered her in our corporate prayers. None of us had met Grandma Olsen, nor were we likely to, and yet we prayed for her and for Kristin, who by chance is so far away from her. We have created a web of concern that wraps around the world. We love Kristin, and that causes prayers to rise halfway across the globe for an eighty-year-old Danish woman.

We take this kind of love for granted. But long hours of vulnerability with one another and a sense of obligation forged our love. Kristin was my student and has told me much about her life. She was a foreigner unable to go home for Christmas or Easter, so we invited her to our home. She housesits for us when we vacation and brings treats to our dog, reminding the dog that she is her best human friend.

She stops by after work sometimes and looks through fashion magazines with our daughter. She is woven into our lives.

Most of us enjoy some solitude from time to time. We get tired of being pulled in many directions, tired of expectations and just tired. We need our downtimes, our routines, some quiet. But for most of us, these times are the exceptions and not the rule. Our lives are rich and meaningful as they are filled with a variety of people. Being alone, having solitude is good. Escaping for a moment from the obligations of social life is great. Being lonely can be terrible.

We have a deep urge to have companionship and community. We need people, and we are obligated to them. That is how I read the story of the creation of Eve in Genesis. Adam is lonely and God gives him a helper, not because he has so much to do that he needs an assistant. In the first creation story God blesses humankind and tells them to multiply and fill the earth. But in the second story, Adam needs someone to fill an aching loneliness that other creatures cannot fill. That person becomes the center of his life, his rib, his love, the one who is so much like him and yet his opposite. They are inextricably bonded together. His undoing is hers. And her undoing is his. They share the garden and the humiliation of expulsion because they try to deceive God. They share joys and they share the consequences of sin.

The story of Adam and Eve is one of the ways love happens. Among the many loves in our lives there is often, but not always, a special person. If we marry or commit ourselves to a partner, we "leave" our parents and cling to this other one, with whom we have a special intimacy, with whom we forge what everyone hopes will be a lifelong, caring relationship.

But we have many loves. We need people to fill our lives. They become the centers of each of our spheres. Life partner, children, parents, siblings, friends, work colleagues, neighbors, and members of our congregations. They are like us and interestingly different. The undoing of our community belongs to us all. We share the garden and the humiliation when we ruin it. We share together the joys of care and compassion and the consequences of deception and sin. We long to have a one true love. But we also need the whole village. For this reason I don't read Genesis in a narrow, individualistic or literal way, as the first marriage, but as God's first invitation, a calling into the love that is the foundation of life together. God's calling into love continues into the New Testament with Jesus summing up all the law into a simply duality. Love God and love your neighbor. Without these loves of all kinds our lives are empty, personally, morally and ethically.

In our backyard in Hannaford lived a family who became dear to us. Their older daughter was close in age to our son and the two played together as we adults played board games or talked together. Heather, the youngest, would let herself into our house whenever she pleased. She knew that I sometimes let butter get soft before dinner on a dish on the counter top. I could always tell that Heather had been there. To her mother's chagrin, and our great amusement, she would let herself into our house, which was almost never locked, reach up, take the butter down, take a big bite off the end and try and replace it. At best, the butter would have little fingerprints and tooth marks on it and be somewhat close to the dish. At worst it was a mangled mess smashed onto the countertop and there were smudges of butter clinging to the walls and cupboards all the way to the door.

One spring Sunday, Heather's family came to church. They sat in the front row of their picturesque country church. Heather was busy with toys, coloring, and taking care of her two-year-old business. When I began to preach she suddenly noticed me. "Momma, it's Mary!" Her mother tried to shush her, which only made her more agitated. She stood up on the pew, looked around at the forty people there, many of whom were relatives, pointed emphatically and called out, "Look! It's Mary!" I stopped the sermon and said, "Hi, Heather." She smiled, and satisfied with the acknowledgment, sat down and went back to her business. They were in that pew nearly every Sunday after that.

Families and their needs form so many of the relationships we enjoy. Among those who do not share our political views and those who experience community in many other ways, we have in common our children, our mothers and fathers, our partners and spouses, our dreams for them, our care for them. We sometimes become close to one another because of our families.

After a few weeks in Hannaford, we had to choose where our five-year-old son would attend Sunday school. We pastored three congregations at first but soon agreed to do interim work in two more that were waiting to interview a new pastor. Then it became impossible to have our kids along with us as we drove from congregation to congregation. Heather's grandmother, who lived on a farm, offered to mind Dan after church every Sunday. Thereafter we dropped him off at their home for church and Sunday school. We were concerned that he would not eat lunch and offend his hosts. He could sometimes pick over his food. So with some concern we picked him up at Marilyn's house. When we came in the door the first time he was devouring potatoes, meat loaf and whatever else Marilyn set in front of him. She was beaming because he was such a "good eater."

We know that we need the people in our community, but sometimes we forget that they need us. The kids were confident of love and care in the little town of Hannaford and even when they were quite small branched out far into the safety of our little neighborhood. Hannah, who was three and enamored of ladybugs and worms, would sometimes run to us. Her eyes pinched closed tightly she would raise her face up, her lips crinkled in a tight buss waiting for us to bend over and give her a kiss. We wondered where she got that little gesture, which was so endearing.

One day I went visiting with her as she made her trip across the yard to see Jo, the neighbor. Jo had been talking recently about her own kids growing up and leaving her. Her mother lived in Iowa. Her husband's parents lived in Canada. "Our lives have gotten so much smaller," she complained. Jo's kitchen was often dusted with flour and crowded with pans as she baked and decorated cakes for weddings and other special events. Hannah sometimes helped her. Jo let us in and Hannah ran to "her chair" in the kitchen, pulled it over and climbed up for a better view of the countertop and began to ask Jo questions. We finally finished our business, and as we left Jo called, "Wait a minute, young lady!" I turned to see Hannah running back and Jo bending over and puckering up for a kiss. Love makes our world so much larger.

I remember as a discouraged junior in college doing a large pile of dishes and then in utter discouragement simply sitting down on the kitchen floor. I could not think what to do to get myself out of my funk. So I called my brother. He was funny and charming and sweet and just what I needed.

One weekend when I was on call as a chaplain, a nurse called. A man had just had knee surgery. The nurse apologized and said that he kept telling staff members that he was dying. They checked all his vital signs over and over and reassured him. Still he insisted he was dying. So they took blood samples and could not find anything. Now he was scaring them. "Sometimes people have told nurses they are dying and then they have a silent heart attack and die," she said. "I know this is very unusual, but would you just come and talk to him and tell us what you think? We don't know what to do next."

Ben lay in his bed and his wife sat in a chair. They were surprised when I came in the door. I introduced myself and told Ben that the nurse had been concerned about him. I asked about his knee.

He slapped the blue cast. "This here is the second surgery on this knee. They stuck in one of those scopes the first time. This time that didn't work. It hurts like . . . . Well, you know. But I'm used to that part of it." He'd had three surgeries on his other knee before this.

"Why did you tell the nurse that you're dying? Has something happened?"

"I just don't know. I just have that feeling this time."

"Was it something somebody said? The doctor or one of the nurses?"

"No, I don't think so."

"But this time it seems different."

He nodded. I asked him to tell me where he was from and a little about him. He had rheumatoid arthritis and it kept his wife pretty busy. I looked at her and she smiled.

"So you've had this a long time."

"Oh yeah. Since I was a kid."

Then he began to tell me about his brother, a Methodist minister. His brother had always come and prayed with him when he was in for these surgeries, but he wasn't planning to come this time because he had services. I thought of the times my siblings could be comforting in ways no one else could.

"He's a big help, I guess when you have all these painful surgeries."

Ben choked up. "I love my brother. He always knows what to say."

"What does he tell you?"

"He just gives me hell if I don't buck up. But he can't come this time."

"Well, let's give him a call and see what he says."

Soon Ben was talking to his brother, his voice relaxed and deepened, and then he listened and nodded for a long time. He burst out laughing. I got up, waved at him and his wife and backed out of the room. He was smiling broadly as he waved back and I knew that the love of his brother was going to help him survive this challenge again. When I checked back to see him two days later, he had already gone home.

Part of loving and being loved in our first years of ministry was our colleagues, a study group. We drove sixty miles and gathered around a table in the fellowship hall of a Lutheran congregation in Carrington. Surrounded with books and papers, we diligently prepared the assigned texts for the next weeks, learned how to preach and do ministry together, and challenged one another theologically and with new models for ministry. We were wholly supportive. We drove nearly every week either to study or socialize with them.

The clergy couple who became our closest friends, Mark and Stephanie, lived ninety miles away. We were friends from the time we were at seminary and stayed with one another many Sunday nights and enjoyed our days off together. We got together and played a silly dice game. I can't even remember how it was played. We made dinner for one another and played the game for hours. Mark and Bob always played against Stephanie and me. We talked about our families and our work. We laughed and sometimes cried, all the time playing the game. Finally we decided that we should keep score, women against men, and play the game of all games to a million points. Mark carefully kept track and wrote the scores on a little piece of paper that he kept in his wallet. It was years before the men finally triumphed.

We needed one another and loved one another deeply. They are still friends with whom I would trust my life and can immediately talk about anything, even though we are now separated by hundreds or thousands of miles and by large gaps of time. In each of our subsequent calls, our colleagues and study groups have been a lifeline for us. Each one has kept us interested in intellectual pursuits, provided us a safe place to be ordinary people and let down our hair, and served as allies in ministry and a sounding board for personal and professional concerns. They have sometimes been our family away from family and helped us in our loving.

Love is mentioned in the Bible nearly 700 times, at least in the translation I just checked. Jesus commands it. It's normal and it is good for our community and us. So one would think love would be easy and happy. But the word "love" itself is problematic. There are so many different kinds of love. The Greeks had different words for erotic love, love between family members, and selfless love. We make it worse. We love our dogs and refrigerators and hairstyles.

Theologians will tell you that love is not only a feeling. More importantly it is an action. It can mean charity or service. Honesty, fidelity, humor, camaraderie, compassion, and hospitality are all ways we show love to one another. We are given to one another for the purpose of loving. Loving one another is not necessarily easy, and we can have many other pleasures, many other purposes in life. But this action, the action of loving, is the greatest of all. This is true. But splitting hairs by defining Christian love as chilly duty in the past has helped me avoid having the heart of God toward others. Jesus' self-sacrificing love was not a plodding duty. He lost everything because he had deep compassion for the world and specifically, for us.

The truth is, love makes us vulnerable and highlights our obligations to other human beings. Love is risky. As soon as we love someone we are aware that we can be rejected or that we might lose them. We no sooner depend on someone than we realize they might leave us. We no sooner give away our hearts than we make ourselves vulnerable to the harm that life can bring, because whatever life brings to someone close to us, it deeply affects us. That is the connection that intimacy and care brings. We are ourselves uniquely, and yet our hearts can be broken. So love makes us vulnerable. When I became less afraid of loss, content even to have that rather than miss my life, I covenanted with God to just allow myself what has always been held out to me but which I did not always take.

So I love my congregation. And when I work with students, I love them dearly, knowing that one day I will lose them because they will go their separate ways. Each person is different. I love that. I love the roots of them, hearing about their parents and communities of origin. I love the leaves and branches, the kids, the friends, the struggles and joys that have made them resilient. I love the fruit, the work, the hopes and dreams. I love hearing about them. I commune them each week and I baptize the little ones with tears in my eyes. I lived into the calling to love. I have wanted to love them all, because none of the other choices are good. It is risky but my life is very full.

I met my partner, Jane, in my second call, which was to a large congregation. We worked together for four years. She was the organist and director of its large music program and she talked me into joining her bell choir. We planned services together and had coffee together many afternoons. We were part of a large group of younger women who celebrated birthdays and commiserated about life. Jane is a gifted and dedicated musician and has worked in three congregations for more than twenty-five years. I admired her and she became a close friend and ally of my family and me.

When Bob and I left that call for an urban congregation, Jane and I realized after some time that we were more than friends. We were overwhelmed with a sense of fear and shock. It was complicated and painful because affection for one another and love for all the other people in our lives collided.

I loved Bob in a fiercely loyal way. In spite of the ordinary and more extraordinary problems a married couple faces, we were together for 17 years. Together we served thirteen congregations, lived in four cities, made friends and gave birth and raised Dan and Hannah. We were friends and colleagues. So I hung on to Bob for several years, knowing what I knew, out of loyalty, because of the vows I had made and for less admirable reasons, such as naiveté and fear and selfishness. I struggled with my own integrity and sanity. I was living a double life. In the end the courage to end the marriage came because I respected and loved him. His vision for our marriage, though quite ordinary, was impossible for me.

The consequences of that decision were a landslide of loss for both of us. But we decided at the outset to support one another financially and emotionally, as we were able. We would not abandon one another or declare war on one another or try to win in some way. We would not put our kids in the middle and we would support one another about parenting decisions as we always had. In other words, in our divorcing we made a conscious choice to love one another. It was a whole new experience of love in my life. We often thank one another for that gift. The closing of the door to our marriage opened others for us. Bob eventually married a friend he met at a retreat center. Jane and I were free to engage in a different kind of relationship with integrity.

During that painful time, I learned that love is a choice. Attraction is not a choice, but love certainly is. Love looks different even between the same individuals as time goes on. One of the things we all had to come to understand was that love sometimes means making the hard decision not to be together. Our parting was excruciating for us and our children were devastated for a time. But now that we are several years on the other side, we can finally say that we are glad.

Bob, my former husband, was getting remarried. We were happy for him, though it was very awkward. One day he came over. Would Jane be willing to help him shop for a shirt for his wedding? Bob is colorblind. He had a certain kind of shirt in mind and didn't think it would take long. Jane and Bob made arrangements and the next day my partner helped my former husband find a suitable shirt for his wedding day.

Hannah complains tongue in cheek that she is too busy on Mother's Day. She prepares three cards and three gifts, to Mom #1, Mom #2 and Mom #3.

Love is not too strong a word to describe what happens between us when we overcome barriers. Bob may often want to kill me, but he loves me. I used to be careful about using that word. Now I think that love is the commerce between us that counts. The ability to love is not a small thing. It is difficult between spouses. It is even more difficult between the rest of us. It is very difficult between those who have every reason to be enemies. And it is like air and water and the earth beneath our feet. And we are called into it over and over again.

Fred died recently. I know his family well. I knew that a granddaughter was to be in a play and wondered if she was missing it. A second granddaughter was beginning a student teaching rotation. I wondered how she was taking care of that. I knew that the third, a close friend of my daughter, was starting basketball season soon. I knew their family story and circumstances that complicated their grief. Fred had been sick for awhile. His wife would be alone. Other siblings lived at a distance and much of the burden would fall on our friends, as it does on children who live close by. Other losses would be remembered, another father's funeral.

As we prepared to attend the funeral, I thought about what a privilege it was to be with them, to know them so well, to be so comfortable with them, to be invited into their most tender time. I thought about how rare in our culture, where so many relationships play on the surface, to know people so deeply, to know about fears and pain and vulnerabilities, to have traveled a significant part of life with them.

In a way I enjoyed the funeral because I heard a great deal about a man who fathered and grandfathered our friend and his children. I felt that we could be helpful in our own unique way, that we had a niche just as other friends and family have one. And I left thinking no matter what might happen, even if after that moment I never saw them again, they are so deeply entwined in our lives that we literally could never forget them.

So we went to Fred's funeral, a wonderful thing in the end. To be invited, to be appreciated, to sit at the table with the family afterward and remain an important part of their lives. It is about belonging and faithfulness and the embodiment of God in community and hope. But mostly it is all about love.

It seems to me that our vision for love among us is often too small. God has loved us, as Grandma said, before we were born, before we "met." That is a very risky and very passionate love. I love my children in that way. I love members of my congregation in that way. I've been called into that kind of love.

Sermon • March 28, 2004

> *Mary took a pound of costly perfume made of pure nard, anointed Jesus' feet, and wiped them with her hair. The house was filled with the fragrance of the perfume* (John 12:3).

I was fifth of six kids, not old enough to count for much, and not the youngest and therefore not so awfully spoiled as my little sister. Fifth of six, part of a pack. The car wasn't big enough for all of us, so we had to catch rides with others to church or to social events. My parents couldn't take us all to special places. We didn't fit, no matter what, so the pack was divided. And sometimes we were left places and my parents didn't notice for hours. My mother loves to tell the story of coming home from church. They couldn't find me after Sunday school, and I was sitting in a rocking chair, just rocking away and singing, all dressed up, four or five years old, just waiting for them to notice. I had been there for two hours. I was just part of a pack.

My grandma lived on the same farm place, and one day she told me something remarkable. "I loved you before I met you." I could hardly believe it. "I loved you before I met you," she said.

I bought a house, which in retrospect is very much like my grandma's house. Wood floors, lots of deep, wood trim, and kitchen cupboards that stick. And even mice, though I'm not at all tolerant of them. Have you had the experience of choosing a home and thinking, "This is it," because of the house itself or the little corner store down the block or the friendly lawn? Our house was kind of a wreck when I bought it. Still, I think it said to me when I walked along the cracked sidewalk up to the door, "I loved you before I met you."

There is a great big birch in our backyard. A fat squirrel, cardinals, crows, a pair of mourning doves and scores of tiny birds sit there. In the summer we spend many pleasant hours under it. In the winter it catches snow and it willingly holds up birdhouses and feeders or decorations if we have a party. It is gracious and says to us, "I loved you before I met you."

Jesus sat at dinner with his beloved friends Mary, Martha and Lazarus. Martha was busy. Mary loved to sit at Jesus' feet and soak up his teaching and his care. They had been through a lot together, these friends. Not so long before this dinner, Lazarus had died. Mary and Martha were disappointed and grieved. Then Jesus had raised a stinky Lazarus from the grave. They'd pulled away the stone and unwrapped his grave clothes and he got up. The authorities were looking for Lazarus to kill him. Now they had dinner together.

There just had to be an aura of fear. Jesus was avoiding some places because of death threats. His friends were threatened too. They all knew what was possible. Jesus' crucifixion was not an unusual event. Thousands of people died on crosses. And there were little factions and some infighting going on. The disciples were vying to be top of the heap. I think some at least probably expected Jesus to be taken away at some point, and they were already wondering who should lead their little movement. So this was a fractious, fearful time.

Then Mary shocked them all by recklessly anointing Jesus' feet with nard. She let down her hair, an offensive thing to do for a nice Jewish girl, and wiped his feet with her hair. You might anoint the head of someone affluent. But feet were repugnant, unclean. It was a waste of perfume that would have cost a year's wages. Immediately, under the guise of social concern, Judas objects. But Mary had met Jesus and learned his lessons of love. "'You shall love the Lord your God with all your heart, and with all your soul, and with all your mind.' This is the greatest and first commandment. And a second is like it: 'You shall love your neighbor as yourself.'" And even, "Love your enemies." So Mary's fear could not contain her expression. Her faith surpassed the reality of the situation. The love of Jesus has the power to extract extravagant love in return. He loved people before he even met them.

All of our Bible readings today are expressions of what happens when people are captured by God's grace. "Do not remember the former things, or consider the things of old," Isaiah says. "I am about to do a new thing... make a way in the wilderness and rivers in the desert," (Isaiah 43:19). People do reckless things when they meet God's grace, things that put their faith over against reality. Paul, after being chased, harassed, threatened, and imprisoned, says, "For Jesus' sake

I have suffered the loss of all things, and I regard them as rubbish...I want to know Christ and the power of his resurrection and the sharing of his sufferings" (Philippians 3:8,10). It isn't that they don't see the reality of the situation. They have been at war with other nations and within their own cultures. It isn't that they ignore reality. They just go beyond it. They provide a vision. They take a very unpopular stand. They say God loves people. They give away everything. They even give away their lives because they are captured by God's grace.

During apartheid there was a long debate within the Lutheran clergy on divestiture of their pension funds from South Africa because of the so-called "prudent man" ruling, which says people in charge of these kinds of funds must make the most responsible and prudent decisions possible. A discussion I attended highlighted their dilemma. Let us say there is a very elderly widow of a retired pastor, named Emma. What would the board do, when they knew that the funds invested in South Africa made money, were a good investment for Emma, and yet supported a government that perpetuated many civil rights abuses? It was not an easy decision ethically, morally or legally. They were caught. They finally set up a new fund, a social responsibility fund that attempts to invest in companies who work above and beyond required measures to engage in just practices. Many of us have chosen to invest there. We were captured by God's grace.

Because of the assassination of Yassin, the Middle East is actually in a bigger mess this week than last week, but I don't even have to talk to people at Christmas Lutheran in Bethlehem to know that they will be there, with their advanced degrees and opportunities to be anywhere else. They provide a vision of peace where there is none. They love Israelis they have never met.

Recently, one of our state legislators, from a relatively conservative rural area, took a stand supporting gay and lesbian civil rights. He told his colleagues that even though this might cause him to lose the next election, he had to vote his conscience. Some representatives from that area wept. Why would he take that risk in such a fear filled time? There are few gay people in his district. He had no reason to vote as he did, they told him. He loved people he had never met.

About a year ago you voted to call a lesbian to be your pastor. It was risky for the congregation. You had to follow the recommendations of the call committee. You didn't know what I was like, what I would say or do, whether the congregation would suffer sanctions, whether many would leave. You loved me before you met me.

A man sat at a table with his friends. Fear was the name of the game. Mary bathed his feet in perfume so that it filled the room. Have you ever taken the scent of a room home with you? Have you ever hugged a friend and taken his scent with you? The fragrance of that room went out into the whole world. Mary prepared Jesus for his burial. A few days later, he died. He loved you, long before he met you.

Called into Laughter

"I know how God makes the clouds move! A remote!"
– Melissa Wilke, age 4, loudly during a church service.

We had just taken a call and moved to Grand Forks, where we bought the home of an elderly woman who had some time before gone into assisted living. It was a wonderful old house that had not been updated in any way in about forty years. It had not even been dusted for months. We decided that we really should not move all of our things until we readied the house in some way for our family. Our children were still quite small, four and six years, so we lived out of suitcases and slept on sleeping bags in our "new" house and stored most of our things for three weeks.

One night Hannah was playing with margarine containers in the bath tub, and I said, "Hannah, won't it be great when we get your bath toys?"

She looked at me with surprise. "Mama, do I get bath toys?"

"Well, yes, Honey. They're put away but soon we'll bring them here."

"We will? I get my boat and Duckie?"

"Of course!"

"Mom, will I get my other toys?"

"Of course you will. We'll have all your things."

"Will we have a bed?"

"Yup, we'll get your bed."

"And mom?" she asked, her body tense and her face filled with excitement, "Will we have a *couch*?"

"We'll have a couch and chairs and tables and everything."

"Don't tell me anymore," she said, clapping her hands over her ears. "It's too exciting!"

My family was large, and something was always happening. Someone was busy in the house with cleaning, cooking, homework, reading, watching television, listening to the radio, singing, playing games or putting together puzzles. We all developed the capacity to concentrate on our own things even in the midst of a dull roar. After supper, weary from a day that began early and ended late, my dad would often fall asleep in his chair, even in the midst of a flurry of activity. One Saturday night, my sisters and I painted his fingernails with red polish while he slept. We giggled our way through the task as he snored. When he woke, we all realized we did not have any polish remover. We scrubbed and tried everything we could think of to get the polish off with no success. He went to church with bright fingernails the next day.

My sister reminded me of this story at a recent family event. As we reminisced about a variety of things we laughed. We laughed so hard that weekend that my sides still ached days later.

One of our goals at mealtime was to make my mother laugh, because once she started, she laughed until tears came. She would always resist at first, trying to maintain adult dignity, which only egged us on. We would tell her stupid jokes we had heard at school that day, make faces or pull silly stunts. One of us would pull down at a corner of one of our eyes with a forefinger, whining, "Mama, would you please remove your umbrella?" and when she looked up, the joker would pull at the other eye, "Thank you."

Part of the legacy in our family was humor. As farm children we worked hard, and my dad encouraged us with good humor and laughter. In difficult times, laughter healed us. It helped us take ourselves a little less seriously. In the midst of heated discussions, it lightened up anger or criticism and opened us to one another. Laughter freed more creative responses. Laughter helped us keep boundaries between work and rest. It cemented relationships between us. Laughter helped us deal with the impossible parts of life.

When my extended family got together, they told stories and laughed. They told many stories of growing up, of interesting people, and of stupid or clever things they did. My great aunts, one of whom is now over one hundred years old, loved to tell stories from their childhood in Sioux City, Iowa. They were second generation Americans, living in a large house with some extended family. For a time, their family cared for two ancient aunts who couldn't speak English. These aunts dressed in black, were quite severe, disliked children and prayed on their knees beside their beds for what seemed like hours. Grandma and her siblings used to lay waiting underneath a dark stairway until the aunts were done praying in the evening, then just as they walked down the steps would reach between the risers and grab their ankles just for the fun of hearing them exclaim in Norwegian, "Herre Gud!" Dear God!

Or maybe the adults would tell a story about a neighbor. One story I remember was about Ron, a fussy farmer.

This was before the advent of herbicides when some weeds were particularly bothersome. Ron drove a disc back and forth one spring day over and over the same little spot of quack grass drinking something out of a brown bag. Near the end of the day he was singing even though he was a quiet old bachelor farmer and wasn't the singing type. For some reason that story really slayed them.

We grew up with laughter as a part of our family legacy. We watched for the comic and absurd. We appreciated lighthearted conversation, enjoyed the antics of little children, and learned to tell stories.

It is easy to bear down and get anxious when our expectations collide with reality. But sometimes God calls us into laughter. In the rough and tumble early stories in Genesis, God called Abraham into a new home and promised him land and as many descendants as stars in the sky. When the promise of having children moved far beyond Abraham and Sarah's reach because of their age, God repeated the promise. First the ninety-nine year old Abraham laughed so hard that he fell to the ground (Genesis 17:17). Later, angels repeated the promise within Sarah's hearing, and she, too, laughed (Genesis 18:12). But soon Sarah had a son, and they named him Isaac, which means "laughter," saying, "God has brought laughter for me; everyone who hears will laugh with me" (Genesis 21:6). The improbable and fantastic are sometimes possible with God. Sarah and Abraham were called into laughter rather than being fearful and anxious.

Learning to laugh at ourselves was key to surviving our early years of ministry. One year, Bob and I decided to order palms for Palm Sunday and lead a procession into worship. To the genuine delight of the five congregations we were serving, some of whom had never had palms on that day, we passed out palm fronds before the service and gathered for a reading and brief liturgy at the door. Then we asked them to encircle the sanctuary and go to their seats. Three congregations had different hymnals for regular use and we forgot to check the tunes. The bright, happy marching music we expected was in a slow minor key in three of the congregations. It worked fine in two places because the organists were skilled and simply substituted the more familiar tune that we expected. But in one small congregation, the substitute organist, coerced by his mother, played the hymns indifferently with one finger in whatever meter and rhythm he chose. Bob describes one of his low points in ministry as an 8:00 worship service in which a few dozen people were trudging around and around the sanctuary bravely waving palms to a lurching dirge.

As a writer for a nationally published women's Bible study, I was invited to present the study in a variety of places around the country. A large congregation in a small town invited all the neighboring churches to join them. It was a long drive on icy roads. When I arrived at the church, exhausted, a nervous woman roared into the parking lot just after me and told me that the town did not have a motel. It was too small. I would stay with Marion who was slightly disabled and was not able to drive. Could I just drive over to her home? I said I would, and the woman who met me sighed with relief, gave me quick directions and roared off again.

I found the house she had indicated, a lovely place on a lake. Marion met me at the door with her finger to her lips. "Quiet," she stage whispered. "Bernie is sleeping." She quickly waved me into a bedroom just to my left and scooted in behind me. "Bernie gets very upset if he's woken from his nap! Don't wake him please. We don't want to make him mad!" She showed me towels and turned down the bed and asked if I was allergic to cats. The cat thought the bedroom was hers. Was I hungry? She would fix a snack. She continued to whisper the whole time. "You might want to keep the door closed at night so Bernie doesn't come in."

Finally I asked with some apprehension, "Who is Bernie?" picturing a mass murderer and thinking that this would be a long night.

"Oh," she laughed and whispered. "That's my husband." She turned and hurried to the kitchen at the end of the hall. I put my things down and followed her slowly. We had a snack together in her beautiful dining room and she whispered the whole time. I confessed I was having a little trouble sometimes hearing her and asked if she had a cold. She told me that she had hurt her voice three years before and had been whispering since.

A man walked into the room wearing a plaid flannel shirt and corduroy trousers. "Here's Bernie," she whispered.

"Hi Bernie," I said, standing and offering my hand.

"This is the lady I was telling you was coming, Bernie. Pastor Albing."

"Huh?" He asked. "Oh." He shook my hand and left.

Marion shook her head and then continued in the conversation where she left off. Bernie rummaged in the refrigerator and disappeared for awhile.

"Is he always so quiet?" I asked, trying to think of what to say.

"Yes, we used to get along so good. We did everything together. But he just never talks to me anymore. And he's angry all the time."

When Marion cleared the table, Bernie came into the family room and sat in a large easy chair reading a magazine. I approached him and sat on the couch. "What's happening in the Times?" I asked.

"Huh?" he looked up. "I can't hear so good," he said.

I raised my voice several notches, and Bernie began to talk. I asked him what folks did in their little town. I yelled at him that I admired the dining room furniture. It was unique and the wood was wonderful.

"I made it," he said.

"You mean the table and chairs?" He nodded. "And the china cupboard?" He nodded again. I was stunned. It was gorgeous. He pointed around the rooms at various tables and other smaller items. "I made all them too."

"You're kidding!"

"C'mon and I'll show you something."

He got up and cheerfully waved at me to follow. I felt a little trepidation, but followed him into the finished basement. I asked about various things there. "Yeah, yeah. I made them too."

He turned his back to me and started to dig in the bookshelves and pulled out a blue three-ring binder. I said something, and he apologized for not hearing. "I was a carpenter all my life and all them power tools took away my hearing," he said.

"Bernie, you're amazing," I hollered, looking around me, and began to ask how he achieved the finish on a bookcase.

"That's nothing," he said waving his hand dismissively. "This is what I wanted to show you. It took me months." He proudly opened the three-ring binder and began to page through it. It displayed pictures of a church's altar, railing and reredos and intricately carved window sashes. He talked about which he had done first, their scale, how he'd solved some of his problems. "This is my church," he said fondly, "not hers. We go to different ones."

"Say," he suddenly brightened, "maybe you can help me with something." We trudged back up the steps into the family room. He pointed at a VCR in a box. "Do you know anything about them things?"

"A little," I yelled.

"Can you hook it up?" He handed me the directions. As I set it up, fixed the time, and showed him what to do, he held a videotape. Finally, he said with some frustration, "I've had this tape of Alaska for three years and haven't been able to watch it."

"You've had the VCR for three years?"

"Yup. And I haven't been able to see this movie of Alaska. It's a place I've always wanted to go." He pushed the start button and watched it begin to run. Then, satisfied, he turned it off. "Well, I can see that in a bit."

Marion came into the room and whispered. "Wow, Bernie is sure talkative tonight."

"Huh?" Bernie said. His eyebrows knit together. Marion didn't respond.

The enormity of their predicament suddenly dawned on me. Marion couldn't talk and Bernie couldn't hear. "Marion," I yelled. "No wonder Bernie gets mad at you. He can never hear you." And I sat down and began to laugh. Bernie joined me. We laughed and laughed. Marion looked confused for a moment. Then she also began to laugh. We talked for a long time that night about how they could become friends again.

We are surrounded by beauty. Art and music and poetry stir us. Our hearts can be filled by many things. Life brings us many, many joys. But often God calls us into laughter even in the midst of difficulty or because of it.

Soon after Jane came to live with us, she arranged for a visit from her mother. She had not had the courage yet to come out to her family. I had known them all for many years, which made some things easier, but others much more complicated. Then her father became ill and died and she did not want to burden them all with more bad news. So she kept our relationship to herself.

Now she hopped into bed, elated and chattering about her plans. She loved to have her mother visit her. She had everything all worked out. There were so many fun things that her mother would love to do in Minneapolis.

Then suddenly she sucked in her breath. "Oh no, Mary!" she wailed.

"What?" I asked, surprised.

"Well, my mother can count!"

"Huh?"

She grabbed my arm and shook me. "She can count, I said! Four people. One, two, three, four. Three beds. One, two, three. Four people. One, two, three, four. Three beds. One, two, three."

"Yup. Your mother can count. In fact, she's very bright."

She held her head with both hands. "Oh, Mary! The jig is up!" Then in spite of herself, she began to laugh. We roared.

We were getting ready for a trip. I had forgotten to do something and was rummaging in the kitchen and complaining about it. Jane's mother and mine were there. Jane's mother said, "That's not so bad. My friend Trudy was getting a ride with her son from Grand Forks to Minneapolis. It's a five-hour drive and they got halfway and she realized she didn't have her suitcase and had to go home and get it." She paused. "Actually, that made me feel a lot better!" We laughed, and then she said, "I'm getting worried about my memory." Mom responded that she had asked me at least ten times how we were going to arrange our clothing in our suitcases for the trip.

"Yes, but I sometimes have to ask Jane ten times when we are leaving for the trip." We laughed together sympathetically. These changes are serious for us, and they will be all right. We will take care of things as they come to us. And we laugh about them. We can laugh because we are so loved and cared for by God and others.

Sometimes our most faithful response is to laugh. God promises amazing things that may seem almost too good to be true. What is funny about us is often what causes us so much sorrow. But, in spite of it all, sometimes our families and our communities and even God call us to laughter.

Sermon • Easter, 2004

Jesus said to her, "Woman, why are you weeping?" (John 20:15).

When my Hannah was only about three, and I was snuggling her into her bed one night, she said out of the blue, "Mom, let's talk about laughing and crying. When do you cry?" To this day, I do not know where that request came from—maybe Mr. Rogers or Sesame Street. Maybe it came out of our concern as 90s parents, that too many kids express themselves with anger and are more numb to the pain of others. So when our kids were little, we talked a great deal about feelings. Maybe it was simply a peculiarity of Hannah, who likes things to be orderly and understandable. At any rate, that's when it all started.

"Mom, let's talk about laughing and crying," she would say when we went for a walk, or when we ate peanut butter and jellies together, or when we drove off for groceries. "When do you cry, Mom?" I'd name as specifically as I could, a time or two when I had cried. And then I would ask her, "And when do you cry, Hannah?"

At various times I told her I cry when I hurt myself. When I fall down. When someone says something that hurts my feelings and makes me feel bad about myself. When I have a bad day. When I had to leave Elsie. When my Grandma died. When Ernie on Sesame Street sings, "On the Moon." When I work a very long time on something or care about something a great deal, and it all goes wrong. When I am afraid. When I am boiling mad. But also, when I am very happy, I told her, I cry. When I laugh very hard, I cry. When I hear or see something beautiful. "When you were born, Hannah," I told her many times, "I cried. Not because I was sad, but because I was so happy."

"So when do you laugh, Mom?" And even though I laugh much more often than I cry, I found it harder to name things. "When you do or say something funny, Hannah. When someone tells a joke. When someone makes a face. When I see a funny animal. When I talk to Mark, I always laugh. When I watch 'I Love Lucy.' When do you laugh, Hannah?" And so it went, for many months. We talked all about laughing and crying endlessly.

It's early Sunday morning. Mary Magdalene, grief stricken, creeps to the tomb after a long and sleepless night. The daylight hasn't yet touched the garden of graves, and she feels her way along the unfamiliar path. When she finds Jesus' tomb, the tall, round stone has been rolled back. Oh, no, his grave has been robbed, she thinks, so she runs for help.

Peter and another disciple come to look for themselves. They bend over and peer into the darkness, see only the linen shroud. It's true. He is gone. In all of the gospel accounts about the resurrection, some of the disciples are worried and disbelieving. When they leave, Mary stands there alone, desolate. It is the last straw. It is terrible to lose a loved one; how much worse to have even his body desecrated, taken from the tomb, denied even that small amount of respect. No place for him to rest, even in death. She bursts into bitter tears. Two angels greet her by asking, "Why are you crying?" She tells her story, and turns and a stranger asks, "Why are you crying?" "Just tell me what you've done with my Lord," she pleads, and Jesus answers, "Mary." And now the tears must have flowed with joy and even with laughter as she recognizes him and says, "Teacher."

Hannah long ago forgot about this game we used to play. But I didn't forget it. We have such mixed feelings so often in life. This morning as you sit here, perhaps with dinner ahead of you, family and friends in the wings, the promise of spring flowers ahead of you, and most of all, the celebration of God's victory over our greatest enemies, sin and hopelessness and death. Even presented with all of this, or perhaps because of this, you may have mixed feelings. You may be more filled with tears than with laughter this Easter morning. It seems to me, and I hope I am not being overly anxious, but it seems to me, that this has been a difficult year for many of you. Not only with the spectacular and tragic events of the war in Iraq and life-killing chaos in Palestine, but the rather less spectacular, but still appalling, personal disasters of personal ill health or the sickness of close friends or relatives, deaths, job loss and grief; with the wearying struggle for civil rights. Some of you may be struggling with the most basic questions of God and life and where you belong. Maybe some of you are so disappointed with this whole religious enterprise that you are only here to please someone else. We're supposed to be happy this morning. And maybe you are. But I'm betting some of you are wondering, "What on earth and in heaven does the resurrection have to do with any of it, with any of our day to day struggles, with home or work or school or our families?" Life goes on, and it's often enough to make the strongest among us weep.

So how do you know? How do you really know what significance the resurrection has? How do you believe this, what the gospel of Luke calls an idle tale? You don't always. You stand there weeping, the evidence of resurrection right before you, and he comes to find you anyway. You are among family in this laughing and crying. You belong to him and he loves you and the whole world. He calls your name. In the most surprising places you will turn and see him and hear his voice.

I heard him in Hannah's questions. In the midst of Hannah's incursion into the world of feelings, we attended my uncle's funeral. We gathered at the funeral home the evening before. Hannah was on my hip, thumb in her mouth and twiddling her ear, tuning in as we thought to some cosmic radio station, as I mingled with friends and family, talking and laughing. I went to the casket to look at my uncle, nearly a twin to my father who was still living at the time. Hannah wondered if he was grandpa, and when I straightened that out, she asked, "What's the matter with him?" He died, I explained. We looked to see who gave all the beautiful flowers, filled with gratitude for the love shown, the tears coming. Hannah had been busy looking around, but with concern on her face she took my cheeks in each of her hands and turned my face to her. "Mommy, why are you crying?" I explained that I loved uncle very much. I would miss him because he died.

Predictably, when we left the funeral home, Hannah said, "Mommy, let's talk about laughing and crying. When do you cry?" And I turned and in a way I saw Jesus and I told her, even though we cried a lot, I felt happy to be with my family; we share a lot and they know me. And even though I was sad about Uncle Herb we also laughed a lot, because we knew he was with Jesus and we would be there too. And one day everybody would be alive again and all be laughing. It was not easy to describe the great mixture of feelings, caught up in the grief of my family, and yet filled with hope and the celebration of a life lovingly and faithfully lived, death and resurrection. Our laughing and crying were all mixed up together. As servants of God we are dying, and see, we are alive; sorrowful, yet always rejoicing; having nothing, and yet possessing everything.

So on this Easter morning, a morning of joy, let's talk about laughing and crying. When do you cry? We crept this week to the tomb in the darkness. Have you had a disappointment? Are you at a confusing crossroad? We peer into the tomb for our Lord and it is empty. Are you grieving today, missing your loved ones? Are you embarking on a new adventure and leaving someone behind? We stand desolate and alone with Mary. Do you feel that you don't belong anywhere? That you can't be home? In frustration and concern we weep. Are you just plain worried and tired? Just tell us where he is laid. Just tell us where to put our faith, our trust. Just tell us where he is.

Out of the morning light, in the midst of music and the confession of the liturgy long a comfort of the church, a voice says, Why are you crying? He is alive. Why are you crying? He has defeated every enemy. Why are you crying? He is among us and among all the suffering of the world right now. He's in Palestine and Iraq. Your loved ones are in his capable hands. Why are you crying? He has a future in mind for you—a new day, a new life, new hope. Why are you crying? He holds out joy for you, and if you are unable to move or even believe, he will carry you. He will one day carry you home.

In Jesus' suffering love, God has defeated every enemy of abundant life.

CHRIST IS RISEN. CHRIST IS RISEN INDEED!

Called into Seeing

A Christian is someone who shares the suffering of God in the world. – Dietrich Bonhoeffer

Several years ago, Larry called the church office in a congregation I was serving. He was the nephew of an older member and was concerned about her. I was on call that day. I didn't know Louise. He said he didn't think she'd been in church for a couple of years. She was now in her late nineties, and he thought she had become more withdrawn. He was her only relative living in the area—his sister lived in Michigan—and he tried to check on her, but he was a farmer, and lived quite a distance away. The day before, she had not let in the man who had been delivering her groceries for a few years, and now Larry was concerned. It took several tries, but I finally did get in to see her. She didn't want to open the door. She told me that she often didn't answer the phone because of solicitors and immediately began to tell me about $10,000 that the bank had stolen from her. She wondered if she was supposed to send money to the church with me. She wondered if that was the reason I was there. No pastor had visited her before, she said.

These were the themes of all of my remaining visits with her. I wondered if she even had $10,000. Her house was miniscule. Dust and cobwebs covered every surface. She had her lawn mowed for her—three times each summer. Each time I visited her over the next two years she wore the same polyester navy dress and the same flesh-colored scarf wrapped tightly around and around her neck. She had been a teacher. This was her mother's house. They didn't have much, so Louise walked to work, three miles, and shared what she had with her mother. I knew teachers' salaries were terrible and their pensions were worse. At one time, Louise knew how to drive, but as the years went by, since they had no car, she sort of forgot how. And now she had to have her groceries delivered. Louise suffered from some form of dementia, so she didn't remember my name, and her illness had given her some paranoia, but she had her past—funny stories about teaching, and not-so-funny stories about getting by on what they had, walking to school over a long bridge in the freezing cold, and a great deal of fear, about people taking advantage of her, the bank stealing, and her niece hoping she died.

I don't know why Louise first allowed me in her door. But as time went on I think she let me in to her home and her heart because she knew that I saw her. We have been called into seeing some who are invisible in society, accompanying them on their journeys for a time, and helping others to see them as well.

One way we express love of neighbor is in working for justice. When we were very small we learned about justice. If we brought cookies to school, we had to bring them for the whole class. It did not matter whether we liked the other person or not. We could not bring cookies and share them with some of the kids and leave others out. On

Valentine's Day everyone got a valentine or no one got a valentine. Most of our parents taught us to play fair, not to bend the rules to our advantage, not to take more than our share, and not to taunt or hurt someone smaller than we were. As we grew older, our parents and teachers and friends expected that we would love one another by being just.

God calls us to more. We understand that we ought to be charitable. Charity is just fine and has its place. But justice is life giving. Charity feeds the stomach, but justice feeds the spirit. Sometimes when we have the attitude of helping others, we take a superior position. The message is that it's just fine to help those poor people over there, but I really don't need to get to know anything about them, or even approve of them. I'll just send something their way so that they can be a little bit more like me and ease my conscience. Helping others often means we are reaching down to them. It implies that we have all the resources, all the power, all the understanding, all that matters in the relationship. We are the bigger ones and the only ones who count.

Instead we are called to see, to see that others' lives are more than the little sliver we may think we know. They are rich in their own ways and invaluable to us. They are our neighbors and deserving of our care. We are just as vulnerable, in the end, and just as obligated to God and the earth and one another. Perhaps that is the difficulty with seeing. We are afraid to see ourselves in their shoes or just to see ourselves.

It was deceit that slithered into the garden and wound around a branch above Eve as she contemplated that fatal apple. She deceived herself first, thinking herself around her own dilemma, then she deceived Adam. Then she tried to deceive God. This is the original sin. In Protestantism it is often defined as arrogance, lust for knowledge, trying to be as great as God is. But deceit encompasses these as well. We are the only ones responsible as adults for practicing the deceit of thinking we are greater than any person or creature. We know rationally that we are not able to be God, but we deceive others and ourselves sometimes without even knowing it. If Eve were asked if she were justified in taking that apple, she could have come up with many good sound reasons for taking it. In fact, she did. Such is the power of deceit.

We have sometimes practiced deceit with Bible passages. We have fought our fears of what would happen if a woman was a pastor or a person of color moved into the house next door by deceiving even ourselves with Bible passages. This often happens in our conversations with and about gay and lesbian persons. How can Levitical laws compete with Jesus' strong injunctions not to judge or the soaring language of 1 Corinthians 13 telling us love is the greatest gift of all? How can we misunderstand Paul's critique of both the Gentiles and the Jews in the first chapters of Romans when we have the little gospel, John 3:16, as a guide? Why do we so seldom talk about passages such as Acts 10 and 11, and Peter's strong belief that the early church was meant to be a blessing to all, that to not welcome others is to test God? The answer is blind deceit.

Instead of helping, instead of thinking ourselves as somewhat better than others, those of us who are claimed by the Living One are called into the humility of accompaniment. We are called into seeing our neighbor, journeying alongside, earnestly discovering the other's gifts, having compassion and trying to learn about the other's pain. Sometimes the one who was love incarnate calls us to see and join our efforts with those who suffer so that they are empowered, and to bless them.

At Lutheran Church of Christ the Redeemer we are working to make our lives congruent with the message of the gospel. As a congregation we are deeply involved in a sister relationship with a Palestinian congregation, Christmas Lutheran. Several times each year members of our congregations visit one another. We support them financially, pray for them often, have served as the liaison for a fundraising effort to repair the organ in their sanctuary, regale our congress people for help, and receive regular updates via email on the social and political realities they face. We walk with them though we are far away.

We are also invested closer to home in advocacy and help for those needing lower cost housing. As a congregation we support a housing advocacy group. One of our members sits on the board of directors. We own a duplex next to our church building and provide low cost housing to two families.

We have also supported and helped raise awareness of organizations ministering to those with HIV/AIDS. In calling me, but also in many other ways, LCCR is vocal about the concerns of lesbian, gay, bisexual and transgender people. We see them. We walk with them. We welcome them. We shelter and befriend them. We bless them.

There are many other people who often slide beneath the radar of society: the poor, homeless, elderly and alone, those who suffer from poor mental health. The list is long. We lift them up and help them to be seen. Part of my life work is sharing with everyone around me my vision for a just world.

My son, a student at a Midwestern university, now hangs a rainbow flag in his room. He was a resident assistant in a dormitory there for some time. Many students applied for a handful of positions. He told me that part of the training and selection process involved polling the thirty students who survived several cuts. They were asked "what if" questions and asked to stand on one side of the room or the other depending how they answered the questions. One question was, "What if you found out your roommate was gay? Would you stay with them?" Dan was one of the two kids who were willing to say yes. He has courageously shared something about his life in spite of the risk of being ridiculed. He sees people.

Hannah, who is now in high school, goes to church even when the rest of the family is on vacation because she picks up Esther, who is 95. Hannah's ministry is to Esther, whose bright spot in the week is worship and conversation at the coffee hour afterward. Hannah sees Esther and loves her.

One summer day Tom came into my office and told me a story. He reminded me that not so long ago he had been wondering if I had any opportunities for him to be a mentor. We had talked at some length and he had left with some viable options to try in the fall. He lives across the street from a residence for at-risk families. Most of those there, he said, are moms with little kids. Tom noticed that the hedge in front of the building was overgrown. So he stopped in the office and offered to trim their hedge. They gladly accepted his offer. Soon one of the counselors came out and asked if he'd like some help picking up the branches. Two young boys raced out of the residence to help. At first they were shy, but soon they were telling all about their families, school, and, he said, how people get old and bald. He told them that as a reward for their hard work, if he could get permission from their mom, he would show them and their mom his train collection that he had begun when he was their age. They could even play with them.

Then, Tom said, it occurred to him that here was his opportunity to be a mentor. "You were telling us to open our eyes on Sunday," he said to me. "All I did was open my eyes and there they were. I didn't have to find them, they came to me. All I had to do was really see them. I just wanted you to know."

The best thing people have done for me, when I was in my most vulnerable and tenuous situations, has been to walk with me. They could not fix the painful things people said and did. But they made my life different by loving me.

LCCR's congregational council asked me to teach the congregation the difference between blessings, civil unions and marriages. So I scheduled a Sunday morning forum. Ours is a small congregation, Sunday school meets at the same time, and the forum is early. Usually there are fifteen participants or, on a good day, perhaps twenty. The morning of this forum, forty-five people squeezed into our small library, including some who had never come before and some people I did not know.

I told them about the differences, some history, and what was at stake for people involved. People offered various opinions, sympathetic to all, and offered some compromises as well. People shared how they had changed over the years. A lesbian couple, members of the congregation, brought another couple, close friends of theirs who are not "churched." At the end of the discussion they thanked everyone for the exciting and welcoming discussion. They said they weren't sure about the whole idea of gay marriage, but they told the group that what they wanted most in life was their love for each other blessed. They felt for the first time that church people had seen and heard them.

Everyone has a "coming out" story, something they wish others didn't know about or care about. Everyone has times when they do not want to be seen, when they feel ashamed to be seen. They anticipate the worst, but often when the thing that troubles us most finally comes into the light it is a profound relief and it becomes what God has intended it to be, a gift.

I have heard this many times from people in different circumstances. So many conversations with people begin, "I have not really known how to tell you this." And then they tell me a story about themselves or their families, about things they have done or things that have been done to them. They come out to me about family addiction or someone close to them who has taken their own life, or that they have a devastating illness. Many of these conversations end with an explanation of how their experiences have allowed God into their lives in a new way, and how they have been blessed and strengthened in their faith.

When I first came out I found a position as a chaplain, a relatively safe place where my supervisors, a Lutheran clergyman and a United Church of Christ pastor and therapist made it plain that I would not be harassed and that they appreciated some of the dimensions of my struggle. They saw me and blessed me. That was a necessary step in "coming out." Someone safe saw me for who I was and still accepted me. They made that particular place safe. But at some point I decided to create my own safety by trusting God. I realized that no one else could do it. My perception that I was at risk in a fundamental way changed as I claimed the safety of God's love for me. That change in perspective was made possible by some people seeing me.

I was at a retreat center. They asked me to be part of a panel discussion about what it was like to be a pastor and be open about being lesbian and partnered. A woman raised her hand and asked, "What do you tell the children in your congregation at LCCR?"

"What do you mean?" I asked, confused.

"What do you tell the children about being lesbian?"

"Oh," I responded, not knowing whether or not she wondered if I somehow encouraged them to be lesbian. "They never ask about it. I don't think they care. They only care that I love them. And I do. And they know it."

The children see me. In the greeting line after a Sunday morning service, proud, smiling parents holding their toddler said, "Jenny said her first sentence this week. Do you know what it was? 'Pastor Mary gives me bread.'" I'm their pastor and they love me.

We should not be surprised that we are all called together into seeing, really seeing, people who are gay, lesbian, bisexual or transgender. But for many this is very difficult. A friend, John, once explained it. We in the United States are mainly immigrants from many parts of the world. It takes two or three generations to finally speak English and understand our own culture. John's ancestors were Scandinavian. Just about the time they thought they were on top of things, they were told they should learn Spanish, and they had to come to accept their Somali son-in-law. But this is what Jesus does. He raises the bar all the time. Expectations of us will always change as the world changes. The Spirit is at work, changing hearts and minds, all the time.

One night, Larry called me. Louise, who had kept so much to herself, had died. He felt uncomfortable rummaging in her house and wanted help in finding something for her to wear for her funeral. I met him there. We went up to her closet. There were two dresses there. The one she always wore, and a new one exactly like it. She had one pair of shoes. Two sets of underwear. And that was it. We buried her and life went on. One day, months later, the church got an official document from a local attorney's office. Louise's estate was to be divided between the church and a country cemetery. Each would receive $350,000.

Those who can be so invisible to us are not necessarily rich in monetary terms. They always offer other riches, if we will only see them, really see them.

Sermon • June 13, 2004

> *Then turning toward the woman, [Jesus] said to Simon, "Do you see this woman? I entered your house; you gave me no water for my feet, but she has bathed my feet with her tears and dried them with her hair. You gave me no kiss, but from the time I came in she has not stopped kissing my feet. You did not anoint my head with oil, but she has anointed my feet with ointment. Therefore, I tell you, her sins, which were many, have been forgiven"* (Luke 7:44-47).

Foot washing was a very important part of Middle Eastern culture at the time of Jesus. Even today, foot washing is an integral part of Muslim ritual washing, which is done before entering a mosque. In Africa, as well, washing feet is important. In rural Madagascar, before class begins, students will often stand in line by a well or a spigot and wait their turn to wash their feet before school begins to prepare for learning.

At the time of Jesus, when someone came to your house, you welcomed them with foot washing as well as a kiss, either on the cheek if they were equal in social standing to you, or on their hand if they were above you in social standing. Then you would have your servant or slave wash your guest's feet. If you did not have a slave, you would provide the water and the guest would wash his or her own feet.

In first century Palestine, these rituals of hospitality were very important. Social standing was very important.

Your behaviors in any social situation either brought shame or honor on you and your family or clan. Every gathering was a chance to bring either shame or honor upon yourself or it was a chance to bring shame or honor to someone else.

Jesus was invited by Simon, a Pharisee, to his home for a meal. The invitation and acceptance were all part of this social shame/honor dance. Simon honored Jesus with the invitation; Jesus honored Simon by accepting. But we find out that Simon had insulted Jesus in a subtle way. He did not meet Jesus at the door, kiss him, or provide for his feet to be washed. Everyone would have noticed and would have been on pins and needles to see how Jesus would respond. Because Simon was shaming Jesus.

It is a part of the politics of power. Jesus had been angering powerful people. He had told the disciples of John that he healed and freed people. He complained to the crowds that when the teetotaling John the Baptist fasted they said he had a demon; but when the Pharisees saw Jesus, they saw a glutton and a drunkard, a friend of tax collectors and sinners! In Luke's gospel Jesus was continually frustrated that the people, especially the authorities, didn't see who he was, and who everyone else was.

Ignoring, not seeing, Jesus come into Simon's house, made him seem small, insignificant. But then, if you are powerful enough, no one else is worth seeing. The Bible is full of these kinds of stories.

When King David wanted a beautiful woman, nothing else mattered. He compelled her to have an affair with him, and then she became pregnant. So he tried to get her husband Uriah home, to cover it up, but Uriah, a good soldier with integrity, wouldn't go home. So in desperation, David sent him to the war front, to be sure he was killed, and then sent a message to the general there not to worry about it. David didn't see Bathsheba's husband, didn't see his own colossal sin. Nathan had to tell him a little parable about a lamb, and say, "You are the man," before David got it at all.

But it is even true of those of us who aren't so wealthy or powerful. One of the most effective ways we use to hurt one another is simply not to see. Even in this congregation, or in our homes, we sometimes know, but we choose not to see.

Simon shamed Jesus by not offering him hospitality. Perhaps the woman saw this, and she rushed in with her little box of alabaster and knelt at his feet and washed them with expensive perfume and her hair, kissing his feet over and over. Simon, and most every Bible commentator, assumed she was a prostitute. No woman but a woman of the night would ever be at a dinner like this. But we don't know if that is true. Jesus had healed so many of so many things, and when he did so, forgave their sin. And she was grateful.

Do you see this woman? Jesus asked. He saw her.

One definition of working for justice might be "calling others to see people." Really see them. Part of our advocacy and accompaniment as a congregation is to help our neighbors, our government and one another see, really see, those in our neighborhoods and around the world who are in need, who are oppressed, who are younger and smaller, poorer or less powerful than we are. So we continue to nurture our relationship with our friends in Palestine. We give two families affordable housing and advocate it for others. We protect children and include them. We pray for Sara and Jonas and their children and for all refugee families separated from their families. We help neighborhood organizations like TRUST keep the elderly independent as long as possible.

Of course I suppose having Jesus see us might not be the best thing. What if we are ashamed of what we have done or who we are? What if the woman hated to have Jesus see who she was, but was so desperate, that she exposed her life, her wounds to him? What if she is like us, sometimes filled with self-hatred for our sins and inadequacies? What if she is like us, grateful for the moments when it sinks into our bones that God cares for us, that Jesus is our friend? What if she got to see first hand the power of his love?

So the woman at the feet of Jesus, in loving extravagance, poured out her costly perfume on his feet and showed him the hospitality his host should have shown him. Jesus saw in her a mirror of himself. He would soon also wash feet; he, too, would pour out something precious —his life—because he loved greatly. "Do you see her?" he asked his host. Do *you* see her? Jesus saw the woman.

In order to get a class discussion going, sociology professor Tony Campolo asked his students what some of the world's great religious leaders might have said about prostitution. The discussion was lively and intense. He was setting up the class to evangelize them, and when the time was ripe, he asked what seemed to be the crucial question, "What do you suppose Jesus would have said to a prostitute?"

He was all primed to point out to the class the compassion and understanding which Jesus had for the colorful women of the night. He was all set to do his best to make Jesus look greater than all the great religious leaders put together. Once again he asked, "What do you think Jesus would have said to a prostitute?"

One of his students answered, "Jesus never met a prostitute." Tony jumped at the opening. He would show this guy a thing or two about Jesus and about the New Testament. "But, he did," he responded. "I'll show you in my Bible where."

The young man interrupted him. "You didn't hear me Doctor, I said Jesus never met a prostitute."

Once again Campolo protested. He started to leaf through its pages searching for those passages which showed Jesus forgiving fallen women. He searched for the place where he gave the woman at the well a chance for spiritual renewal.

Once again the student spoke out, this time with a touch of indignation in his raised voice. "You're not listening to what I am saying. I am saying that Jesus never met a prostitute. Do you think that when he looked at Mary Magdalene he saw a prostitute? Do you think he saw whores when he looked at women like her? Doctor, I don't think Jesus ever met a prostitute."

Friends, do you think that when Jesus looks at you he sees a recovering alcoholic? A gay person? Someone who cannot be forgiven for an error, an accident? An old person or a young person? An abuse victim? A loser? Someone who can't get it right? Or even a winner? I don't think so. I think when he looks at you he sees a beloved child of God. I think when he looks at you, in a way, he looks into a mirror and sees himself. He sees you, and in that seeing is redemption. I think when Jesus sees you, he sees the one he loves without exception. I think he hopes that you open your eyes too, and really see. And I think these things are things everyone around you could stand to hear—and see.

Called into Vocation

What will she do the rest of the week? – Christine Wilke, age 9, upon hearing that her aunt was going to be a pastor.

Early in my ministry I was asked back to Luther Seminary to preach at a professor's tenure installation. I had been her teaching assistant, and when she was tenured she decided to invite one of her former students to preach. I was excited and terrified. I carefully prepared the sermon in the midst of two busy weeks. I would preach on a Monday morning. So we took care of our services Sunday, visited two hospitalized people and attended a birthday party. Then we packed our suitcases, toys and all we would need for a five and a half-hour trip in the car with two little ones. We were delayed several times and finally left in a rush after five o'clock.

When we got to Minneapolis we discovered that we had left my suitcase lying on the bed at home. It was eleven o'clock at night. No stores were open, nor would there be anything open the next morning in time to purchase something before the ten o'clock chapel service. I borrowed a dress and shoes, both a size too big. I stuffed Kleenex in the toes of the shoes, put a belt around the middle of the dress and borrowed an alb and stole. Aside from a little caution and one little stumble the service went well enough. I only had to totter five feet to the pulpit.

My professor opened a window for me into myself. I realized that I loved to preach. I loved to study the assigned Bible texts, get the sense of them, ask questions of myself and those around me and those voices that we find in books and magazines and other resources. I loved to play with the ideas, listen to those who would be hearing me, imagine their questions. I loved choosing certain kinds of language, trying to make the stories and the context come alive. I loved watching for the themes and sense of the text in the daily interactions of those around me. I especially loved finding God's voice of grace each week. It was a comfort and challenge to me. Even as I prepared to speak to others, God spoke to me. I loved to preach.

A prominent member of the Hannaford community died. He had been a state legislator for many years, and his heart stopped while he was out dancing with his wife in the nearest large town. The month before, one of his grandchildren was baptized. We gathered with his large family at his home. He and his wife hosted a generous buffet lunch, boisterous conversation, and high humor. Afterwards, he was on his hands and knees in the living room, in the midst of his guests, with grandchildren playing horsy and clinging to his back. Then he lay on the floor, tossing them up into the air. On his face and in his eyes was adoration of his children and grandchildren and when time came to make a speech for those present, his faith and his love came through in quantity. Three hundred people were present for the funeral in a church that held one hundred and fifty. I told stories as I preached of his faithfulness to his family, church and the wider community, of the gifts that were his in his baptism, and the reassurance of reunion one day with all those he loved.

Afterward, at the luncheon in the basement, a young man came up to me, introduced himself as an attorney on the deceased's staff, and asked where I got the funeral sermon. I told him I had written it the night before.

"Yes," he said more distinctly, as though I was a little slow, "I realize you wrote what you said today, but where did you get it?" I explained once again that I had written it. I got the texts from the Bible.

"Yes, but surely you have books that you people use for the basics, the outline of it, and the stories." I once again explained that I didn't use anything except the Bible.

This was not entirely accurate. I did tell a story. It was a community story, a faith story, and a family story, which for me joins the stream of the Bible. I preached our tradition, the living tradition, of a loving God among us. At the center of my preaching is the living Word. This is not my doing. I think it helps to be as prepared as possible, but if preachers won't do it, God finds ways to let people know about grace and the power of sacrificial love and care for the whole community, particularly its most vulnerable members. I suppose if we didn't get up and preach "even the stones would cry out."

One of the things I enjoy most about parish life is preaching. But I delight in many things about it. My work is varied and uses all different kinds of skills and creativity. In one week I am a public speaker, leader of community worship, advocate for the poor and oppressed, writer, musician, teacher, interpreter of the holy, counselor and friend. I meet many people and come to deeply know the folks I see every week. They are all different ages, have different sorts of problems. They carry with them interesting stories that I love to hear. I enjoy discovering how they came to be where they are, what their passions are in life. Part of my call is to love them and I do.

I am called heart and soul to be a pastor. This in itself has been a long journey. For me, it was a call into integrity as well as into vocation. For a long time I did what was expected of me and did not consider what I might enjoy doing. I didn't look at the world and think, "What would I love to do when I grow up?" Instead I asked, "What ought I do?" The answer to that was what others valued in me. The loudest voices won me over, the ones that enjoyed my music, the ones that always wished they had become teachers. So I taught music for a few years and my dissatisfaction grew in spite of putting a great deal of energy into my teaching and having success. I again answered the question "What ought I do?" and left after a short time. I felt tired and bored and lonely and thought law school would be stimulating.

Wherever I lived I was deeply involved in my local congregation. At the time I entered law school, I was doing what I always did. I was directing a children's choir, was a frequent Sunday morning assisting minister, was on worship committee and church council, and even filled in for the secretary when she had to be away at the same time as I was taking classes. Once again my dissatisfaction with my vocational choice fatigued me and filled me with frustration. The pastor of my congregation heard me out and then drove me to Luther Seminary in St. Paul and introduced me around because he saw in my dedication as a lay person love of the church and the aptitude to be a pastor. I still did not take to heart a pastoral call. That discernment evolved for me over time.

Of course, being interested in the work of the church and working many volunteer hours does not necessarily mean that a person is headed toward the ministry of Word and Sacrament. All believers are ministers and have a vocation, a call from God into service of God and neighbor and the world. In my Lutheran denomination we say we are a "priesthood of all believers."

Bertha helped every Friday with a fellowship for retired and elderly members, some of whom couldn't come to Sunday worship. Volunteers picked up the participants in cars, vans, and buses. Some of the funeral directors in town sent around a driver to pick up people in limos. And Bertha always served. She came at least an hour early, started the large coffee urn and helped prepare a lunch of sandwiches. One of the pastors on staff conducted a short communion service, and then everyone sat down to have lunch together. Bertha was both unremarkable and remarkable in how faithful she was.

Bertha, like Mary, is a symbol of the church, bearing Christ to the world. Just as Mary carried the Holy One, so did Bertha. With careful steps she walked from the sacristy, where she slowly poured the wine into the tiny glass cups and prepared the wafers on the paten, down to the old altar. Just as Mary gave herself in hospitality, so Bertha greeted all the people warmly. Just as Mary provided nurture and care to the infant Jesus, so Bertha cared for the elderly and infirm, provided lunch and comfort to each. Just as Mary sang a powerful song of justice, of the lowly being lifted up and filled with good things, so Bertha lifted up those in the community who were brought low by the difficulties of living to an old age. In all those ways Bertha was the bearer of Christ. She embodied the church in that place in her own way.

So did Guy. I met him when his mother, Dodi, died. She was a member of one of the congregations we served as interim ministers. We didn't know her. We had just begun our ministry that day. There had not been a pastor there with a regular call for two years. Guy called and I met with him. He told me that when his mother's death was imminent he took vacation and stayed with her for a few weeks. She was a devout woman. Guy picked up her worn Bible and read her a psalm or another passage several times a day. They conversed when she was able. The last day she was alive she sat up, which she had not done in days. Guy asked her what she would like to hear. She said she would like to hear Psalm 23. He sat beside her and began to read. "The Lord is my shepherd.... Even though I walk through the valley of the shadow of death.... Surely goodness and mercy shall follow me all the days of my life." Guy said that the two of them imagined her into heaven that day. She was walking in green pastures. She was sitting at the banquet table and the goodness and mercy would have no end. They imagined themselves back together again one day, in heaven. What would they do? What would they say? Guy ministered to her, and then she said she was tired. She lay down, slipped into a coma and died.

People are called into vocations of all kinds and use their gifts in many ways. Fred Johnson was the mayor of a small town in North Dakota. He was very gruff, owned a construction company, was the only guy in town (I think) with his business' name lettered on the side of his truck. He had an eighth grade education, wore Carhart blues, those all-in-one coveralls, with "Fred" embroidered on the pocket. He was foul-mouthed, drank hard, and everyone complained endlessly about him and re-elected him. He was also a member of one of our congregations. One spring day I found a fair-sized hole in the churchyard, about eight inches across, that hadn't been there in the fall. I found Bob and we surveyed the situation, wondering if a badger had made a new home, or if this was the place all the snakes were living. I wasn't sure what all the possibilities even were. He picked up a big stick. I stood back and he shoved it into the hole and couldn't find the bottom. I found stones, dropped them one by one, and we put our ears close to the ground and didn't hear them hit the bottom. We determined that we'd either found the hole our mothers told us about that went down to China, or it was an old well. We didn't know whom to call. So we called Fred. He said he'd be right there.

Within a half-hour he was backing into the yard with a truckload of gravel. His able assistant, who looked to be about thirteen years old, was already raising the front of the dump truck as he backed up. Fred slid out of the passenger side, talking to us the whole while in a loud voice, punctuated with many expletives. He fastened a chute to the back of the truck as he still talked, opened the gate and in two minutes unloaded a half a truck of gravel, smiled and drove away. Bob and I were left standing guard over that hole, in a sort of daze, thinking about it. Fred, in his very ordinary way, had probably saved a child's life that day. He would have said that he wasn't big into morality, compassion, integrity or ethics. He certainly wouldn't have called this his vocation. He saw a need and just took care of it. I could tell that he loved getting up in the morning and going to work.

Recently an evangelist told a group of which I was a part that if we are not uncomfortable we do not have a call. A call hurts, he said. I don't believe that is how we are called. I think God gifts us, prepares us to bless others, loves us into reaching out in our own particular ways, and once we know it and experience the freedom and joy of it, we will be willing to endure almost anything to be in that place. That is how the Apostle Paul describes his call. He is willing to endure anything, he calls everything he has lost and suffered rubbish, so that he can do this thing God has called him to do.

I am called heart and soul to be a pastor. So when I came out as a lesbian to family and friends I thought I had lost my vocation and it was an unimaginable grief. There would be no place for me as a pastor in my denomination. An enormous part of my life was simply gone. How could God so carefully prepare me, use my gifts, give me a place that I love and then take it away? I consoled myself by immersing myself as a layperson in a local congregation. I sang in choirs, played instruments and made it my habit to encourage the paid and volunteer staff there. I took training in chaplaincy and was called to a position as oncology chaplain. I began to teach seminary students clinical pastoral education.

God did not take my vocation away. God continued to work and prepare me. I was able to live out my call in a different way, amongst those with cancer and with pain, and with students who were gaining the skills to be ministers in a variety of settings. I accompanied them in their sojourn in a strange land, even as I was on my own journey toward life. My work was compelling and fulfilling and I loved it. But I missed the parish.

Many gay and lesbian persons in many church organizations are still waiting for an opportunity to be pastors. We have, as a group, laid aside plans, or taken other kinds of positions in congregations, or set aside our personal lives and relationships. But our calls do not subside, because they are not entirely about gifts or choice. They are not about rosters. They are about what we love. They are about a fire that the Holy Spirit has begun in us. God continues to beckon us and to teach us and to console us.

I was talking about discovering what we love with my sixty-year-old friend. She has had the same job for thirty years and has loved it. But now she is looking ahead to a new vocation. She hopes it will be something entirely new and is looking forward to a new discovery—a discovery of what she loves. I'm convinced she will not so much find it as God will open it to her if she just asks herself, What do I love to do? Who will God have me bless?

I have a call into what I do. Part of it is the particular gifts I have been born with and skills I have developed to speak and organize, to lead people in song and prayer, to write and manage. Part of it is that I enjoy people and find them interesting. I appreciate their differences, their foibles. Part of my call is wanting to do it, having the heart for it, and possessing the love of it. But a large part of it is inexplicable and moves as the Spirit of God moves.

Sermon • October 26, 2003

> "*You will know the truth and the truth will set you free*" (John 8:32).

I bring three questions about this gospel reading to you. First, what is it to be a slave? Second, what is it to know the truth? And finally, what is it to be free?

First. What is it to be free? The Jews said to Jesus, "We are descendants of Abraham and have never been slaves to anyone." HUH? The Hebrew Bible is filled with stories about Israel's and Judah's domination by others. They began their history in slavery in Egypt. Finally, they got to the Promised Land, after which though they enjoyed some periods of prosperity, their neighbors in the Middle East, like Egypt and Assyria, Babylon and Persia, romped back and forth over them many times. And finally, Babylon dragged them off into exile. Then in the time of Jesus, Rome had its foot on their neck. What do they mean, they've never been slaves?

We might respond to Jesus the same way, "We've never been slaves to anyone." Though segments of our society have experienced slavery, and some have been prisoners of war or of our own state, sitting in prison, the vast majority of us have never been in bondage, at least not in physical bondage. But all the same, most of us have experienced slavery. In fact what has often been presented to us as freedom is in fact slavery.

We tend to define freedom as an absence of boundaries or duty. Doing what we please when we please. Recently a letter to the editor of the local paper responded to a long commentary on people driving around those waiting at construction zones. This man wrote defending his own breaking into line saying it gave him an extra 20 minutes with his kids every night. At first I thought it was a satirc or a joke, then I realized he was serious. He had no thought that anyone else waiting in that long line might want to spend time with his or her family. Freedom means having nothing to tie us down or get in the way of self-gratification. We do not want to hear that our wealth or power obligates us to others, or that we need to live within boundaries. Many, if not most, people in our society would say freedom involves enjoying every crumb of what we have earned to do with as we please.

So we have had a tendency to push the boundaries of freedom. And in each way that we do so, it has had a profound effect on our life together, from road rage to a lack of reasonable self-discipline and simple civility to our tolerance of violence and war. In pushing our freedom we have become slaves to our self-indulgence and violence. Though we have been the freest nation in the world, it could be argued that we are also the most enslaved in the entire world. We ought to know that doing what we please when we please isn't freedom at all. It's a lie. We are slaves in many ways. But just like the Jews, who told Jesus that they were never slaves, we blindly say we are free.

Jesus says, "You will know the truth and the truth will make you free." So my second question is "What is it to know the truth?"

The truth is, we are all human and we are in this together—not something we like to admit. We like to take on more than we can handle and work until we almost drop. We like to manipulate others and hang onto injustices, to collect them and pay them back later. We like to cover up our feelings and weaknesses. We think we can go it alone. We like to pretend that we will live forever. In short, we like to forget that we are human. We would rather be God. Sometimes a little warning light shines into our darkness. This week I attended the funeral of a young man, Pete Erickson, only 33 years old, and I wondered what might be said at my funeral. Have you ever wondered about that? What is the truth? The truth is that we are human, very weak, and very needy and that one day people will be eulogizing us in our own funeral service.

But there is another side to this truth that Jesus holds up. And that is himself. He is the truth. The truth is that God so loved the world. God is love. We are limited and sin because we are human, but God's disposition toward us is revealed as gracious. So when we come to know Jesus as pure love, we will know the truth.

So given our limitations, here is my third question: what is it to be free? Today we celebrate the Reformation. One definition of Reformation is truth telling. When we speak the truth, things change personally, as a congregation, in our society, in the church. As Martin Luther pounded those 95 theses onto a door nearly 500 years ago, I don't think he had any idea what that truth would do and how much trouble he would discover. You in this congregation know that when you tell the truth not everyone is overjoyed.

Jesus says, you will know the truth and the truth will make you free. Freedom is the presence of truth. And that truth is Christ, and the love of God. But freedom in Christ is also binding ourselves to him, becoming slaves to Christ and to love for him or others. So what does the truth do? Free us or bind us?

Martin Luther states it well when he said, "A Christian is a perfectly free lord of all, subject to none. A Christian is a perfectly dutiful servant of all, subject to all."

We will always have the structures of physical and moral limitations. The commandments are summed up as loving God and loving neighbor. The truth is we need one another and we need God, and we act as though that is not true. We blatantly and inadvertently hurt one another. We need one another and are vulnerable to everyone's sins toward us as well. We must care for one another or we will not survive. That is what it is to be human and live in community, but it is not an impossible situation because Christ has redeemed our human condition. Now to be human is not to be in an unacceptable, intractable position, it is not to be a slave to sin because Jesus took on human form and became human. Now to be human is to be a child of God, human still, but an heir of the realm of God. Then what has become so burdensome for us we are able to do out of love. Inside this physical and moral condition, we may have the freedom of Christ. Both Lord of all, and servant of all.

Our family has had many pets. We have two dogs and two cockatiels, but for a long time I had canaries. When Dan and Hannah were young I bought a canary and let them name it. They were very young, and I was prepared for anything. They insisted on calling it a very creative name, Bird. Shortly after we got Bird he had some sort of aviation accident in the middle of the night and caught one toe in the door of the cage and hung upside down all night. I was surprised that he lived at all, but he was injured. One little leg stood out straight from his side. Not a good thing, and eventually his toes all fell off. But he lived for years, balancing on his one good leg and a stump, happily singing. I ended up adopting another canary, a female. And since we had Bird, we called her Birdette. Birdette always was nesting... in the food dish. She sat there patiently night and day. Now if you're wondering, Mary, where are you going with this, just hear me out.

One day I stuck a piece of lettuce between the wires of Bird's cage and sat down to eat my breakfast. Lettuce to a canary is like caviar to a Russian or lefse to a Norsk or aebleskiver to a Dane or—you fill in the blank. But I had accidentally put the lettuce where Bird had to stretch to reach it, which is a problem because he had only one foot. He was hopping sideways and leaning, then fluttering and regrouping to try from a new spot, the lettuce always just out of reach. After quite a long time, he finally managed to get one succulent bit of lettuce. Then rather than eating it, he hopped across the cage and fed it to his mate, who was of course, sitting in the food dish.

Freedom as God intends is different than the kind of freedom our society offers. It is freedom to be the people that God intended. Free to be human, free to make mistakes and ask for forgiveness, free to be the church that tells the truth, and free to serve others, giving them our best, not just our leftovers.

Today I offer you this image of freedom. A bird. Not so much the great eagle whooshing over the tree tops, but Bird. Living within his physical limitations, inside a cage, and still offering the richest tidbit to the one with whom he shares his bondage.

Freedom for a Christian is binding oneself to the assurance of God's grace as we stand in our own space and tell the truth, on the one hand, perfectly free. And at the same time, not condemning but caring for our brothers and sisters everywhere, perfectly dutiful. Our place is reserved for us no matter what today or tomorrow may bring. As children of God you have a place in the household of God. So if the Son makes you free, you will be free indeed. Free to fly. Free to serve. May it be so. Amen.

Called into Hope and Courage

I always sleep with my bedside light on, in case I should die in the middle of the night. – Elsie on strategies for living alone.

One day, Sally, a cancer patient, requested that a chaplain bring Communion, and I brought it to her. The hospital was full that day and there was a curtain pulled between Sally and the woman in the other bed, Susan, who had been newly admitted. Sally had specifically asked for confession, and so I pulled up a chair in that crowded space between the curtain and the narrow bed. Speaking in a low voice I began the familiar words "…we confess that we are in bondage to sin and cannot free ourselves. We have sinned against you in thought, word and deed, by what we have done and by what we have left undone." After absolution I continued with a short gospel reading and then with the remembering: Jesus at the table with the disciples, the eating and drinking. "For you for the forgiveness of sins."

I realized that Susan, who I could not see behind the curtain, was weeping. So when I finished, I asked if it would be all right if I visited with her. She said she would like that and could she also have Communion. I repeated the little service I had just done and then she told me a story. She had not had communion for twenty years. She was raised Lutheran and she married a man who owned a tavern in a small town. So they were up very late on Saturdays and it was hard to get to church. Still they did their best and always sent their three kids.

Things went well until the kids got into confirmation and there was a new pastor who insisted not only that the kids attend worship, but the parents as well. When Susan and her husband missed some services, they were taken to task and their daughter was kicked out of confirmation. They quit the church, and even though she thought she should have found an alternative, she felt cut off, separated, less than the others. She was angry for years at both the church and God, so she stayed away. But in cutting herself off from judgment she had also cut off a part of her life that was important to her. Now she had cancer. Her doctor told her she would live a year, and she was frightened. So when she overheard confession, the words of Jesus, the Lord's prayer, her faith was re-membered, and she was both cut to the heart and at the same time felt the sheer grace of God. We continued to meet over the next months, and her conversations with God gave her courage to face what lay ahead.

I met an attractive woman, Margaret, who had cancer in her cheek. The side of her face was disfigured with surgery and radiation and she felt ugly. It was a very rare cancer, which left her feeling alone and afraid, and she could no longer talk without difficulty and pain.

One day she came in to see me. She was always a composed woman, wore suits, had now cut down her workweek to forty hours. That day she began to sniffle and then sob. She was afraid. I wondered with her how she had gotten through all the rest of what she'd been through. She showed me the cross hanging around her neck. She was a Christian, but now she was afraid of dying. She wondered how could that be? Her husband was supportive and loving. She had no money worries, but she was terrified. She wanted to know what it would be like to die.

Eventually, through the American Cancer Society, she was connected with a person with the same type of cancer, so they could support one another. He was in hospice. She brought him flowers and ran away in terror the first time she met him and then was deeply ashamed. She came and talked to me. I wondered if she was being given the opportunity to meet her own death in him, and I encouraged her to go back and tell him she was afraid. She did and he was touched and understood. They talked for a long time that day, and she visited him many times. Her fear and her ability to be vulnerable with it paved the way to a new relationship. Her cross, often in her hand, gave her courage to assent both to her own death and to the life that blossomed between her and her new friend.

God calls us into hope and courage. Oftentimes, in the midst of the challenges of life, a moment comes in which there is a recognition, a baptism, an opening, through which we realize that we are able to walk into whatever might come. In that moment someone gives us a gift and in the gift we see the hand of God reaching out to us to help us through whatever might come.

Pastor Kvamme gathered my family before my grandmother's funeral. He ushered us into a small side chapel smelling of Lemon Pledge and mildew. We sat on hard, red velvet covered chairs made for tall Scandinavians and my sister and I fidgeted until our mother leaned forward in her chair down the row and stared at us meaningfully. I looked past Pastor at the stained glass windows picturing scenes from the life of Jesus. Pastor witnessed to us what we already knew of our grandmother—her hard life, her unswerving faithfulness, her service to others—what was true, noble, just, pure, lovely, gracious virtuous and praiseworthy in a Christian. Then he read for us a passage she requested that he read to her family: "Rejoice in the Lord always. Again I will say, rejoice. Make your reasonableness known to all people. The Lord is near. Be anxious about nothing but in all things by prayer and supplication with thanksgiving let your requests be made known to God. And the peace of God which exceeds all things will guard your heart and thoughts in Christ Jesus" (Philippians 4:4-7).

What an odd thing to have read to the family at a funeral service, I thought. How could we rejoice in the face of such loss? How could we not be anxious in the face of death and the absence of an important member of our family? And how could we live up to the expectations of such a text which expects truth, nobility, justice, purity, loveliness, graciousness? It took me a long time to say a gracious farewell to Grandma, but in that time, Pastor Kvamme and Grandma gave me that text to carry with me.

My uncle chose the hymns for his funeral. As we followed his casket, our throats closing over our grief, we sang "Joyful, Joyful, We Adore Thee." In this way we celebràted his life even as we wished he were still with us. Everyone approaches illness, loss, grief and death in their own ways. People make sense of their lives as best they can according to their own life stories, their own gifts and ways of being. Uncle gave us a great gift that day, a hymn of joy, and within that hymn of joy was the gift of hope so that we could live with courage even as we grieved.

I have leaned many times on the gift of Philippians from my grandmother. She knew that we often have a hard time in farewells and was trying to equip us for the journey of life as best she knew how—in these few words from Paul. "Rejoice in the Lord always . . . . Be reasonable before all. Turn your anxieties over to God and concentrate on the fruits of the Spirit, including truth, nobility, justice, purity, loveliness, and graciousness." These are words for the journey. She knew that our good-byes are a part of life, but do not extinguish it, that even death was not a final goodbye, but ultimately cause for rejoicing. And that the peace of God which exceeds all things would guard our hearts and minds.

A man was causing a great deal of trouble for the hospital staff in the intensive care unit. He would not leave his wife's side. Ed was telling the hospital staff that something was wrong. He knew it because he knew her so well. Nurses had encouraged him to go home, but he refused. The chaplain was called to mediate, to convince him to go home and rest. Tim went to the bedside and Ed began to tell him how his wife was changing. He urgently begged him to help. So Tim paged the attending physician who discovered that Ed's wife was silently bleeding internally. Without his watchfulness she would have died.

Later, when she returned from surgery, Tim talked to Ed once again. Ed told him how he had been standing in the driveway when his ten-year-old son chased a soccer ball into traffic and was killed. "I didn't watch him," he said with tears in his eyes, and with renewed determination in his voice, turned to look Tim straight in the eyes. "I will never make that mistake again. I didn't watch, so I will always watch her," he turned and nodded toward his wife.

Ed was called into hope and courage. He had made a mistake, but the mistake did not defeat him. Instead, in that moment he was called into hope that would allay his paralyzing fear, and he was called into the courage to stand up for his wife when she was not able to speak for herself.

For several years I had assumed that I would never be in public ministry again. I left a parish call in order to spare that congregation and my former husband grief. I entered chaplaincy, hoping that in specialized ministry I would not be noticed and that my call would still be fulfilled in that setting. To a great extent, as I met people at the lowest and highest points in their lives, as they shared their lives with me, I was able to do so. At a certain point, when I had simply had enough, I decided not to let fear determine my life. Then I was called in an entirely different direction, into hope. I decided to act like I belonged, so I filled out papers requesting a change of call. In those papers I once again informed a bishop that I was lesbian and intended to be partnered.

I was called into courage and hope. At the same time, a congregation called Lutheran Church of Christ the Redeemer had decided to take a stand and had opened the door to calling a gay or lesbian pastor. They had nearly finished their process of choosing a pastor, but agreed to interview me. The outcome was that three months after submitting my papers I had a call to that congregation.

I was in a state of distress because I didn't know if it was a good idea to go there or not. I had taken a strong stand, but I didn't want to destroy anything. The reason I'd left my previous call was that the congregation had not asked for a lesbian minister. It wasn't fair to them to harm them in any way. This was a different situation. The congregation was prepared. They had acted on their congregational constitution through a thoughtful process. I didn't want to take a commitment to people who were so lovely for granted. So I thought about it and prayed about it for many days. I had many conversations with old and trusted friends.

Dan is an old—and conservative—friend from my study group on the North Dakota prairies. He came into my office one day at the end of the day. A parishioner of his was undergoing heart surgery. We talked about that for a while. He told me about taking a new call and his personal pain about his decision to become a pastor in another church. We talked about his call in his congregation and what he liked about it. And we talked about his family and mine. He asked after my former husband who was also a good friend of his and how he was doing in his ministry.

A few days later there was an article about my call to Christ the Redeemer in a local denominational paper. Shortly after that Dan was back in my office at the end of the day. I waffled for awhile, my insides in a whirl. I just didn't know if he knew I was lesbian. I wondered if he'd read the paper. We talked for awhile about many different kinds of things. Finally he asked me if I'd accepted that call. I confessed that I had.

"What do you think of it, Dan?"

"Well, God bless you," he said with a kind of laugh. "What will happen to you?"

"I'd be put on leave from call until the churchwide meeting makes some kind of decision."

All my thoughts and feelings spilled out to this trusted old friend even though I was no longer certain what he thought of me. I told him about my circumstances, how I'd loved the parish and how meaningful my work in the hospital was, but how impatient I was beginning to feel because I missed using my creativity. While not easy, I had loved going to work every day as a pastor. So I told him that there was a day in November I felt I was being pushed out of what I had been doing, though it had been good for me, and called into the parish again. And I told him that I am who I am and still feel I belong. I went on about wanting to keep my integrity.

I told him about Jane, that I have someone who lives with me whom I love very much. She cares for my children and me, upholds my former husband with love and care, welcomes all these difficult parts of my life and understands what it is to be in public ministry since she has worked her whole life in the church. I said I'd reached a point where I was tired of being afraid and tired of not doing what I'm best at, what I love doing and what I feel God has called me to do.

I explained that I felt our denominational policy that banned partnered gay clergy was unjust and that the documents that we accede to that deal with sexuality cannot be reconciled. On the one hand it asks me, as a called and ordained person, to uphold justice for all people, and on the other hand it asks me to agree to something that is unjust to me. I confessed my fear that when I had sent in my papers I would be removed from the Lutheran clergy roster, but I was tired of being afraid, that I finally felt I had healed enough from all the bumps and bruises to have a little courage again.

I told the long story of how Lutheran Church of Christ the Redeemer, a congregation in Minneapolis, was looking for a new pastor. They opposed the Lutheran church's policy of excluding partnered gay people from the list of possibilities. Many of them have gay friends or children and they had come to believe that excluding gay leadership is wrong. But by the time I'd gone in to see the bishop, the congregation's call process was nearly finished. I'd been in contact with the chair of the committee, who, when I was finally able to submit my materials to the congregational committee, brought the materials to the committee. They were nearly finished with their call process by the time they got my materials. So she told me she didn't know if the committee, who had already met many hours, would be willing to even read my resume. I told her I understood and was glad that they were there. It helped me to know that there was actually a congregation out there who was willing to call someone who was lesbian and partnered.

When they got my materials they reluctantly decided to interview me. One member of the committee told me later, "We were tired. I hoped you were really weird so that we could quickly reject you." And I told Dan that I got the materials about the congregation at 5:00 one day and had to interview at 7:00, that I didn't think I had enough time to know them well enough to even ask intelligent questions. I was sure they would not want me for many reasons, but after all of our corporate uneasiness, when we met we were all excited, thinking it could work. I took time to discern, and in the end, against all odds I thought I would go. I was ninety percent sure.

Dan studied me. Dan was the one in our first text study group out in the middle of North Dakota who, when the youth group was growing or a sermon went well, reminded us, "This is the work of God." He kept our feet to the fire, made sure we preached what God was doing. So he helped me enormously in the way I prepare sermons and do my ministry. I have never forgotten. He listened to my long story about how the congregation and I almost missed one another and about all of the coincidences I described, and he said, "Mary, this isn't coincidence. This is the work of the Spirit. It's a call from God."

With tears in my eyes I said, "Each time I see someone from my former life, it's difficult. Each time I worry how

I'll be received, what the comment will be, how we'll be together. I didn't want to alienate you."

Dan said, "You could never alienate me. You're right here in my heart." He patted his chest. "You're my friend and nothing will ever change that. Back when we were pastors on the prairies you taught me how to be a pastor." I told him I had been thinking the same thing. And he blessed me.

I went home and I sat at the kitchen table, as Jane and I often do at the end of a long day. When she asked me how my day had gone, and I tried to tell her about that conversation, I wept for the second time that day. It was one of those moments of recognition. Dan gave me a gift, the confirmation of my call that I needed from one who is for me, and always has been, a messenger of God's grace. He was the voice of God calling me into hope and courage.

Hope and courage are the endpoint of this part of my journey. In a way, they are not such great accomplishments or even the end. I choose to occupy my space on the face of the earth. But in another way, they are accomplishments. They are the accomplishments of the Holy Spirit finally getting through to me, teaching me to embrace for myself what I have known all along for others. And they are not the end.

My nephew was recently married. Many family members were gathered. Some of us were sitting around a table at the noisy reception. My brother and his wife, anticipating an "empty nest," had taken ballroom dancing lessons, and remarkably (at least to me), they were leading the dancing in the center of the room. My dad's cousin, whom I hadn't seen in a few years and who is fighting cancer, badly wanted pictures of everyone. I held my breath since so often in "family pictures" Jane and I are not put together. "Hannah, go stand by your mom." Camera in hand, she waved her around the table toward Jane and me. "Lean in, you two," she waved me closer toward Jane. "I want a picture of your whole family."

Things change. We are called into new ways of being.

God so loved the world. . . .

Talk at Central Lutheran• April 2003

I'm a mom to Hannah and Dan, and I'm a sister to five good people. I'm an aunt and a daughter to a patient woman. I have many friends. I'm a work colleague. I'm a mentor. I have many committed relationships. And I live with Jane, who is in my mind, and in all practical ways, my spouse. I have many committed relationships but I am sometimes identified in the community by one.

I am a writer and public speaker, a counselor and comforter. I help reconcile relationships. I help people find meaning in their tragedies. I'm a planner, and I'm an advocate. I am a pastor, and that means I've been called in all these specific ways to bear the living Word of love and hope.

Between Jane and me, we have been serving the church in paid positions for nearly 50 years. We've given our adult working lives, and our hearts, to the church. And yet there are many who would like to exclude us because we are so different.

And for good reason. When I get up in the morning, I make coffee. Then we take the dog for a walk, with our coffee. And then I shower and we have breakfast. Sometimes my 16-year-old daughter and I are doing her trigonometry by 7 in the morning, and, let's face it, that is very strange. Then I drop Hannah at South High and go to work, and I teach chaplain students and talk with people who have cancer and pain. Then I often have a commitment here at Central. Then I go home and clean house or watch TV. And then things get really exciting for me. I get to go to bed and go to sleep. I'm exhausted. I'm sure that's quite a lot different than any straight person. And I should know, because I lived that way for many years.

I was married in 1983 and ordained in 1988. I was married for 17 years and served three calls with my former husband Bob as a clergy couple. But when I was 40, I discovered I was gay. I spent two years considering it, finally telling Bob. We were colleagues and friends and I still feel very protective of him. He is a great human being. At first we didn't know how it would go; we thought maybe we could make it work for a while, at least until the kids were out of school or something like that. But reality soon set in. It was unworkable because it was a mockery of our understanding of marriage. So we decided to part.

This first decision was terrible. We were both the first in our families to divorce. So I began the painful and often humiliating process of coming out to people. We thought this out together, sat down the kids one day, then told family members, then met with the bishop. By that time I was at Abbott Northwestern hospital doing a CPE residency so that I could become a chaplain. The bishop accompanied Bob as he talked to the congregational council where we served, then we talked to more friends, and on it went. Friends recommended various attorneys for our divorce. We decided divorce did not have to be adversarial and promised to be advocates for one another. We helped one another with the paperwork and made agreements about various things. Bob helped me buy a house. I will help him do the same when he needs to. He remarried. Jane came to live with me. We support them. They support us. We know that we are very blessed.

Someone asked me, "How could you suddenly decide to be gay when you're 40? That's a good question. Something I asked myself until I was crazy and depressed with it. I went into therapy because I thought, I must be wrong. So people ask how could that happen—often in an unkind way —and my real answer is "I don't know." And that is, for me, a relatively self-aware person, humiliating.

But that utter humiliation was only the beginning, because in a way, every relationship changes when you come out, and nearly every touchstone of self identity and community identity changes as well. And with those changes come extraordinary losses. My circumstances and decisions caused lots of sadness around me. My Hannah, who was 13, burst into tears and said, "I thought we were happy!" It took time before our relationships felt settled with her, and she is once again content. My mother was disappointed because Bob was one of her favorite people. A close friend told me she hoped I suffered. I divorced, moved, changed jobs, changed my friendship circle, changed my status with many groups of people, changed where I worshipped and my role in worship all in one year. I felt I made many choices, but that much of my life was simply taken away from me. I loved parish ministry, liked going to work every single day, and felt that I would never be able to do it again. I experienced all these changes, at least at first, as loss. If you imagine life as something you put together, like a little block structure, taller and stronger through life, mine was in a large pile of rubble, and I had to rebuild, reconstruct all these different parts of my life. I have to say that the one thing I did not lose in the midst of it was my belief that God loved me, though I was sometimes doubtful about the benevolence of many human beings. Coming out was by far the hardest work I've ever done. No one would wake up one morning and think, "Gee, I think today I'll become gay. That would be fun."

But time heals many wounds, and I am absolutely surrounded by loving, encouraging people: Jane, our close circle of friends, my family, many people at Central and people at Abbott Northwestern. I have learned through my own experience and my experiences in chaplaincy that the living Word really is among us and in fact *is us* to one another when we are able to be loving. That incarnational God is the only God who makes sense to those who suffer acutely.

This last fall I missed preaching, the creative aspects of parish life, the long-term relationships and the chances to do social justice in so many ways. One of the authors I go to when I need solace is Wayne Muller. His admonition is that vocation is all about what you love, so just do what you love, no matter the cost. For me, the bottom line about God, the guiding principle, the heart of the Bible, and the end, if you will, of our relationship with God, is love. God so loved the world. Only fear keeps us from knowing it, embracing it, teaching it, and including in it everyone we meet. We get so scared that we don't even know we're scared. I no longer wanted fear to be the way I made my decisions. So I listened to friends and my own heart and decided to go back into parish ministry.

At the exact same time, Lutheran Church of Christ the Redeemer was looking for a pastor. My decision required a visit with our new bishop because of our denominational policies. He was very kind, but requested that I go on leave from call until the status of gay pastors is determined. It's a long story, but all of this took time, and LCCR and I almost missed one another. I am so honored and humbled that they have called me. After consideration, I knew it was the right thing.

It's taken time to mend, to build, to dream. But I decided in the end that I'm Lutheran and a pastor. This is my tribe. I am just as broken, just as humiliated by life circumstances, just as vulnerable as everyone else is. I belong here. Someone will have to throw me out, and they may. But I will not live half a life. God calls me, and all of us together, to much more.

[1] The Rediscovery of Anguish, Peter B. Vaill, from *Rediscoering the Soul of Business*" ed. DeFoore, p. 70.